TOP HATS AND SERVANTS' TALES

A century of life on Somerleyton Estate

———————ை ை———————

Ann Gander

———————ை ை———————

First published 1998 by Holm Oak Publishing
St Michaels, Narrow Way, Wenhaston, Suffolk IP19 9EJ
Telephone: (01502)478702

Copyright 1998, Ann Gander

A CIP Record for this book is available from
the British Cataloguing in Publication Data Office

ISBN 0 9533406 00

─────────── ∽ ∾ ───────────

CONDITIONS OF SALE

Typeset by Karen Kohn

Printed in England by PMT Print
Unit 6 Sarum Complex, Salisbury Road, Uxbridge, Middlesex

Photographs by Ford Jenkins, Lowestoft; David Bartram, Chelmsford;
photograph of Phyllis, Lady Somerleyton page 55 by kind permission of
London Illustrated News.

For
Mum and Dad

Contents

Acknowledgements

I should like to thank all those who have helped in the preparation of this book, by providing information or sharing their precious memories.

In particular, my thanks are due to Lord Somerleyton for allowing me access to his family archives, and to the Honourable Mrs Mary Birkbeck for her wealth of information about the family and their staff.

I am deeply grateful to all those former employees of the Somerleyton Estate who willingly recalled their days in service and to the families of those who are no longer with us for lending me memoirs, diaries and photographs. I should like to remember two special people who have passed on since I started the book – Bertie Butcher, a remarkable man with enough stories to fill a book of his own, and Violette Beechener, a dear, modest lady who has been reunited with William.

A large number of organisations have freely provided research material or help and I am indebted to them. They include Eton College Library; the Imperial War Museum; the National Army Museum, Chelsea; the Regimental Museum of the 9th Lancers, Derby City Council; the British Red Cross and in particular the Lowestoft Record Office.

I am grateful for the gracious permission of Her Majesty the Queen for the use of material from the Royal Archives.

My thanks are due to the following for granting permission to use extracts from their publications:
Frank Prochaska, Philanthropy and the Hospitals of London, 1992 by permission of Oxford University Press; Lesley Lewis, The Private Life of a Country House, reprinted 1997 by Sutton Publishing in association with the National Trust; Jessica Gerard, Country House Life – Family and Servants, 1815-1914 published by Blackwell Publishers; Frank Cullum for permission to quote from his book Both Sides of the Fence; Geoff Howes for Valentine Quartet; Eastern Counties Newspapers; Reverend Jonathan Riviere, Rector of Somerleyton for permission to quote from old parish newsletters and to Nick Lee, descendant of Kerry Rix, for permission to quote from the diary of Kathleen Rix.

My thanks also to Trevor Gower for generously sharing so much of his own hard-earned research on Somerleyton families, and to Emma Clemens, curator of the Somerleyton Hall artifacts, who has become a treasured friend. For tireless support and encouragement I should like to thank Fiona Clarke, Lord Somerleyton's private secretary, also Robert Malster for invaluable advice, and a big thank you to Jim Hayward for giving enormous encouragement and constructive criticism.

Finally I should like to express my deep appreciation to my husband and children for their patient support during the past two years.

PART ONE

Top Hats

THE CROSSLEYS OF SOMERLEYTON

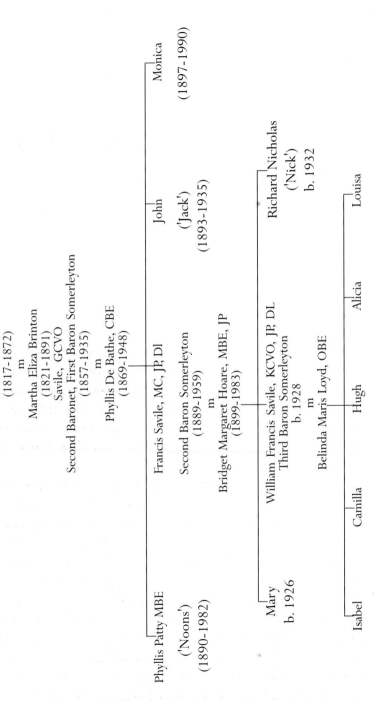

Sir Francis
First Baronet
(1817-1872)
m
Martha Eliza Brinton
(1821-1891)
Savile, GCVO
Second Baronet, First Baron Somerleyton
(1857-1935)
m
Phyllis De Bathe, CBE
(1869-1948)

Phyllis Patty MBE

('Noons')
(1890-1982)

Francis Savile, MC, JP, Dl

Second Baron Somerleyton
(1889-1959)
m
Bridget Margaret Hoare, MBE, JP
(1899-1983)

John

('Jack')
(1893-1935)

Monica

(1897-1990)

Mary
b. 1926

William Francis Savile, KCVO, JP, DL
Third Baron Somerleyton
b. 1928
m
Belinda Maris Loyd, OBE

Richard Nicholas
('Nick')
b. 1932

Isabel

Camilla

Hugh

Alicia

Louisa

Chapter 1

From Halifax to Somerleyton

W hen Savile Brinton Crossley came into the world on June 14th 1857 half the people of Halifax had cause to celebrate. His father Francis, known locally as Frank, was one of the famous and respected Crossley brothers who had helped shape the Yorkshire town with their charity and enterprise. Theirs was the biggest of all the burgeoning carpet mills, soon it would become the greatest in the world, employing thousands of local men, women and children.

Frank was a true Victorian philanthropist who even went so far as to say it gave him more pleasure to share his money out than to earn it. His pride and happiness that day came from one of the few things his great wealth couldn't buy. It was also a relief for Frank to have a son and heir at last, as he and Martha had been married for twelve years and so far had been childless. But he wasn't about to stand still and hand out cigars, he had work to do.

Frank was in the midst of creating a new gift for the people of Halifax, a park where they could go after work and unwind in tranquil surroundings. He had been inspired by a trip to America where he saw the stunning panorama of a mountain wilderness, and he wanted to share some of the joys of nature with those who had little hope of ever escaping the rank, smoke-laden air of their home town. At times it had seemed an impossible task but he was adamant that God himself was the driving force behind the scheme, and Frank was determined to move earth, rock and water to achieve his dream.

At the ceremony to open the People's Park in August 1857 Frank Crossley said that while this wasn't the proudest day of his life, it was the happiest. In a long speech his biography spilled out as he paid tribute to his family's humble roots. His mother, a farmer's daughter, had been in service and his father a carpet weaver before finding fortune in the mechanised loom. Of the many Crossley mottoes, he felt that one above all others had special meaning and that was his mother's vow 'If the Lord does bless us at this place, the poor shall taste of it.' He had kept that promise time and again, and this was just the latest scheme to benefit the less fortunate. The Park had cost him £40,000.

Frank described his mother as a tough, spirited woman and it is clear that he had looked for the same qualities when choosing a wife. Martha Eliza Brinton, a carpet weaver's daughter from Kidderminster, was no great beauty, although she was attractive in a homely way. Her family had wealth but she had never craved fashion or trinkets, and this aspect of her nature appealed to Frank, who despised foppishness and frothy follies. But Martha was smart in other ways and she could fight her corner when it came to the defence of her loved ones. It was she who would be blamed as much as credited for his purchase of Somerleyton Hall.

Family lore says Martha wanted to leave Halifax because it didn't fit in with her social aspirations. It has been claimed that she fancied herself in the grandiose mansion in Suffolk rather than their own modest villa in a smoky northern manufacturing town. This seems a might unfair when there are so many clues to suggest that Martha's insistence on moving was not for selfish reasons at all.

Her husband was nothing less than a workaholic. He was often away on business, leaving his family at home in their house named Belle Vue. There they were surrounded by a cemetery, the Crossley-built almshouses and the Crossley-founded People's Park whilst their neighbour was a man who had annoyed Frank by refusing to sell his property for an extension to the garden of Belle Vue. Frank's response had been to block out the offender by building an impressive, battlemented wall complete with gothic watchtower.

Home was now their castle but such had been the impact of the Crossleys on their town that reminders of their success were everywhere and there was even a street named after them. Frank, a portly man who exuded energy, was driven to maintain the trend, going into the works at every opportunity or discussing work, or, being the 'brains' of the business, planning new moves. When the stress began to take its toll his doctors said he must retire and not in or near Halifax. Their message was blunt - if he did not get away from it all he would soon be laid to rest there.

Francis Crossley

In 1861 Frank, then in his 45th year, saw an opportunity to please his wife and doctors and also to benefit a friend in need. Fellow MP Sir Samuel Morton Peto, known as 'the maker of Lowestoft' for his massive investment and construction works in the Suffolk town, was in serious financial trouble. Peto had capitalised on the advent of the railway and created a trail of tracks across Britain and faraway lands but ambition had run away with him and his wealth was on a rapid decline. The jewel in his personal adornment had been the Somerleyton Estate. Since his purchase he had virtually rebuilt the whole village and he had 'preserved' the modest Elizabethan hall. In fact he had enlarged and altered it beyond recognition, sparing no expense in the creation of his Italianate dream home. Now he would have to give it up and the sale catalogue, with adjectives as fancy as the masonry on the hall itself, declared that the 'Princely Residence' and entire estate would go under the hammer in July 1861.

SECOND EDITION

IN THE COUNTIES OF SUFFOLK & NORFOLK.

PARTICULARS

OF

The Somerleyton Hall Estate,

COMPRISING A

MAGNIFICENT FREEHOLD RESIDENTIAL PROPERTY,

SITUATE MIDWAY BETWEEN LOWESTOFT AND YARMOUTH:

IT CONSISTS OF A

MANSION,

With a grand Elevation, exhibiting one of the finest Examples of **Anglo-Italian Architecture** to be met with in the Kingdom,

AND HAVING

AN EXTENSIVE AND ELEGANT WINTER GARDEN,

With many other Luxurious Adjuncts,

SURROUNDED BY A

Finely-timbered Park,

IN THE CENTRE OF A

NOBLE AND UNINTERRUPTED DOMAIN

OF

NEARLY 3,300 ACRES,

DIVIDED INTO EXCELLENT

AGRICULTURAL HOLDINGS, with superior HOMESTEADS;

Interspersed with fine PLANTATIONS and WOODLANDS, extensive LAKES, and a DECOY,
with its beautifully-secluded Waters, presenting numerous enjoyable features;

NEARLY THE WHOLE OF THE VILLAGE OF SOMERLEYTON;

EXTENSIVE & VALUABLE DETACHED ESTATES;

EMBRACING, WITH THE MAIN ESTATE,

About 4,450 Acres,

Presenting a SOUND LANDED INVESTMENT, united to the CHOICEST RESIDENTIAL FEATURES:

ALSO,

VARIOUS IMPORTANT PROPERTIES

In the TOWN & PORT OF LOWESTOFT, and in the MARINE SUBURBS,

Giving, with the Somerleyton Estate and its detached Lands,

An Annual Rental of £10,603,

EXCLUSIVE OF THE MANSION:

FOR SALE BY AUCTION,

BY

Messrs. DANIEL SMITH, SON, & OAKLEY,

AT THE MART, NEAR THE BANK OF ENGLAND,

On TUESDAY, the 16th day of JULY, 1861,

AT TWELVE O'CLOCK,

AS AN ENTIRETY, IN ONE LOT.

Particulars, with Lithographic Views of the Mansion and Plans of the Estate, 10s. 6d. each, may be had of Messrs. SWIFT, WAGSTAFF, & BLENKINSOP, Solicitors, 32, Great George Street; of Messrs. TAYLOR, MASON, & TAYLOR, Solicitors, Furnival's Inn, E.C.; of Messrs. NORTON & REEVE, Solicitors, Lowestoft; and of Messrs. DANIEL SMITH, SON, & OAKLEY, Land Agents and Surveyors, 10, Waterloo Place, Pall Mall, S.W.

ALSO,

With trifling exception,

THE ENTIRE VILLAGE OF SOMERLEYTON,

With its Picturesque Green, on which are erected, in form of a Crescent,

TWENTY-EIGHT COTTAGE RESIDENCES,

Of a most Substantial and a highly Ornamental character—showing, in the Domestic Arrangement and in the Sleeping Apartments, a singular and rare attention to the comfort and morality of Peasant Families;

SEVERAL

PRIVATE DWELLING HOUSES,

AND VARIOUS VILLAGE PROPERTIES,

In excellent general Repair.

THE PERPETUAL ADVOWSON AND NEXT PRESENTATION

TO THE

Rectory of Somerleyton,

The Tithes of which are commuted at £850, exclusive of Glebe Lands;

TOGETHER WITH

EXTENSIVE MANORS OR LORDSHIPS,

WITH ALL THE

RIGHTS, PRIVILEGES, AND EMOLUMENTS

APPERTAINING THERETO.

Leased for a Term of 21 Years, of which 10 will be unexpired on the 1st of March, 1861, *at £400 per Annum, determinable in* 1864.

The Somerleyton Estate

IS SITUATED IN A DESIRABLE PART OF THE COUNTY OF SUFFOLK,

ABOUT FIVE MILES FROM LOWESTOFT,

RAPIDLY GROWING INTO A FASHIONABLE & SELECT SEA-SIDE RESORT;

SEVEN MILES FROM GREAT YARMOUTH, also a FAVOURITE WATERING PLACE;

TWENTY MILES FROM THE CITY OF NORWICH,

With easy transit to the Metropolis by the East Suffolk Line of Railway, and a Navigable Communication with the Harbours of Lowestoft, Yarmouth, and Norwich, by means of the Rivers Waveney and Yare,

OF GREAT COMMERCIAL IMPORTANCE TO THE PROPERTY.

A private deal was struck but it was not until two years later that Frank, Martha and little Savile moved into Somerleyton Hall. That was a particularly good year for Frank who was then knighted and became Sir Francis Crossley. An article in the Bradford Weekly Telegraph would later suggest that the family had turned its back on Halifax after the purchase of the Somerleyton Estate. In truth Sir Francis stayed loyal to the town, remaining an MP for the area until his death. His speeches were not considered brilliant, but he did throw everything into them in his passion for civil and religious freedom.

Frank could surely be forgiven for enjoying some of his hard earned money, considering he gave so much of it away. Somerleyton Hall was a fitting treat for Martha too, allowing her the chance to forget about the Crossley carpet empire just once in a while. It was a honeycomb of splendid rooms filled with myriad works of art, many of which had been commissioned or collected by Sir Morton Peto. There was a cavernous banqueting hall complete with organ gallery, an oak-panelled parlour reminiscent of the original Elizabethan house and newer rooms for relaxing, entertaining, working and playing. There were bedrooms fit to accommodate a king and at the very top of the house, basic but adequate quarters for dozens of servants.

In good weather the family and guests could wander the rolling parkland, or on dull days they could bask in the artificial warmth of the winter garden, a soaring glass conservatory with tropical plants and handsome statues. If that were not enough, the estate amounted to over 3,000 acres including Somerleyton village with its charming cottages under mops of thatch and the picturesque school, its diamond-paned windows winking in the clear East Anglian light. Everywhere they went the Crossleys were greeted with restrained nods and curtseys of respect from the shy but naturally curious tenants and employees. The locals were used to self-made squires by now, but the broad Yorkshire accent took some getting used to.

Sir Francis admired it all and nodded with satisfaction at his wife's pleasure, but even Somerleyton Hall didn't have the power to tie him down. Travelling between Halifax, London and Suffolk, he ignored all advice and kept up his former pace. Sadly then, his enjoyment of the status, wealth and popularity he had amassed would last less than a decade.

In 1869, when Frank knew that he was losing his battle for health he determined to make a pilgrimage to the Holy Land. He set off with Lady Crossley and a medical attendant but could not get beyond Rome. Returning home almost an invalid he was forced to rest in the tranquillity of Somerleyton. Still he managed to do some business and even appeared at the House of Commons. At the end of 1871 he returned to Halifax in a very frail condition and delivered a speech in church, concluding, 'I have known men who set their hearts on money, and the bank broke and their hearts broke. Set your hearts, friends, on Christ. He won't break and your hearts won't break. I am not able to say more. Goodnight.'

Sir Francis Crossley's heart couldn't take any more strain. In January 1872 it gave up the struggle after just 55 years.

Yours Truly
Francis Crossley

In accordance with his wishes, Frank was buried in the Crossley family vault at Halifax. His widow and son retreated to Somerleyton Hall. Young Savile was only fourteen when his father died and he hardly knew the man he had just lost. Frank had sent the boy off to private school, determined that he should have the best possible education, and they had rarely spent time together. Now Savile would have to find another father figure to help him towards manhood, but it would not be a member of the Crossley family. His mother was about to wage war on her in-laws.

The widowed Lady Crossley

As was common, Savile's inheritance was put into the hands of trustees. The idea was so that young sons could not squander their fortune before they were old enough to appreciate it. However it would not be Dame Martha who held control. Not until the 1882 Married Woman's Property Act could wives be deemed fit to enter their own contracts, so instead the bulk of Sir Francis' estate was handed over to his brother John Crossley and nephews Edward, Louis and Henry Crossley and Benjamin Musgrave. The latter had been a business adviser to Sir Francis and was thought to be a canny caretaker of the legacy, worth over £1 million.

Martha still had the right to live at Somerleyton Hall with an allowance of £6,000 a year and she could keep her personal clothes, jewels, horses and carriages, food and wines. Apart from these few essentials she had virtually no say or stake in her late husband's property. She could sell any fixtures, furniture or household goods only on condition that she replace them with items of equal value and an inventory was taken at an early stage. Everything had to be insured out of her own money, in return for which she could continue to enjoy the grand hall and its contents.

Nevertheless, Dame Martha was not the sort of woman to sit back and admire the view. While Savile was back at Eton she entered into a bitter dispute with the trustees of the estate over their handling of Sir Francis' affairs. The Crossleys and Benjamin Musgrave had been left to manage the money as outlined in the will but they had invested it largely in the Crossley carpet firm of which they were all directors. It grieved Martha to find that all this had happened when £23,500 was still owed for the Halifax orphanage and there was a mortgage of £90,000 outstanding on Somerleyton Estate. There seemed to be no provision made for honouring these agreements.

Letters galloped back and forth over the next two years, with the Dowager Lady Crossley insisting that the unsecured loan to John Crossley & Sons Ltd of over £250,000 should be invested elsewhere, and the two debts paid. The trustees argued that the money was tied up, although they did settle the orphanage debt. Meanwhile they secured most of the loan by taking debentures from the company but otherwise steadfastly maintained that their actions were legal and in the spirit of Sir Francis' will. Martha took the matter to the High Court.

With no legal claim on the property herself, she arranged for young Savile's interest to be represented by a friend. The Bill of Complaint was filed at the Chancery Division of the High Court in May 1874 and the following year a decree was issued that the mortgage must be cleared. Martha had won her case but her tenacity had made her most unpopular with her in-laws. Now she had even less desire to visit Halifax, the town that she felt had contributed to her husband's death, so instead she immersed herself in life at Somerleyton.

The serenity of life in Suffolk seemed to bring out the softer, more sociable side of Dame Martha, as witnessed in this anecdote written by a late villager, Bob Farrow, 'I am a twin, born 1879 at the South Lodge on Lowestoft Road. Father was at that time a groom at the hall stables. Lady Martha, Dowager Crossley, called on my mother to see the babes. She was so pleased she asked my mother if she would name us Francis and Robert after her late husband and her brother. She often came to see us. I remember a wickerwork pram which she sent for our use, also a lot of clothes and books and toys.'

Martha was kind to her employees, and appreciated their loyalty. Her trusty servants Mary Sherwood and Ann Bedford had moved from Halifax to be housekeeper and housemaid at the hall and Mary's daughter Elizabeth was the teenage cook. The butler, Charles Howes of nearby Belton became a long-standing tower of calm strength and Kerry Rix was the estate agent, the pivot around which the Somerleyton wheels of industry would revolve for many years. A battalion of gardeners, woodsmen and farm labourers kept up with the changing seasons on the estate and the colourful characters knew the meaning of hard work and spare-time enterprise. They would turn their hand to all kinds of work and they found extra income wherever they could, whether that might be pumping water for the larger houses in the village, or mending shoes, cutting hair, or killing rats. For many years James Hurley received £1 a month just for winding all the hall's clocks each day, in addition to his normal work as an engineer on the estate.

Dame Martha felt very much at home among these people. They were honest and hardworking - almost every waking minute was devoted to feeding and clothing their large families. They found light relief at the Duke's Head pub, or in sports such as football and cricket, and dances at the village hall offered the younger villagers a chance to find themselves a partner for life. At the turn of the century, with limited means of travel and few social opportunities, it was natural that locals would meet and marry near home. More than one couple found the first flush of romance while waiting to fill their buckets at the village pump.

Clearly there was a friendly atmosphere among the close-knit staff on Somerleyton Estate - agent Kerry Rix married the hall cook, Elizabeth, and she and her mother Mary Sherwood, the housekeeper, left their jobs to go and live with Kerry in his estate cottage. Charles Howes, the butler, married the sewing maid, another Elizabeth, and in later generations footmen and gardeners would tie the knot with maids from the hall.

Meanwhile the number of live-in staff at the hall increased steadily and

Extract from the Somerleyton accounts

by 1881 a number of local girls and women had been taken on. There was a new housekeeper overseeing four housemaids, also a lady's maid, cook, kitchen and scullery maids, and a footman and groom living in the servants' quarters. Still there was room for plenty more in the spacious attics. The butler lived in a cottage nearby but he had a makeshift bed in his pantry for those occasions when his services would be needed well into the night, and the ranks of hall windows would blaze with lamplight, fuelled by gas from its own gasometer.

For life certainly did go on at Somerleyton after the death of Sir Francis. Whisky and soda was brought in by the gallon and oysters and wine purchased to supplement the bounty of meat, fruit and vegetables reaped from the estate. There were shooting parties and soirees for which Dame Martha made shopping trips to Harvey Nicholls in London or ordered silks for gowns to be made by her seamstress.

Whenever Savile came home he could be found hunting, shooting and fishing or roving the estate, learning about the ways of the Suffolk countryside and the Suffolk countryfolk. It was a relief for him to cast off the starchy uniform of a young gentleman student and roam with men who had the country in their heart and bones. These were people who would swap clothes with a scarecrow if it had on a decent jacket and trousers, in contrast to Savile's upper-class schoolmates who wouldn't be seen dead in less than the best.

Savile sometimes found his school life decidedly dull. At Eton his education was mostly classical, chanting and dissecting Latin and Greek verse with little variety and even less enthusiasm. However, there was scope for the boys to follow outdoor pursuits such as riding, rowing or shooting and Savile became more than adept at all three. It was also outside the classroom that he learned some valuable social lessons.

Savile was an attractive young man, he was not tall but he had arresting blue eyes and a pleasant aquiline profile, and he was always keen to take part in outdoor sports. He was undoubtedly popular but he was not elected to Pop, the college's elite social and debating society, and he did not win any major prizes. Nevertheless, while rubbing shoulders with future judges, generals and politicians he developed a nimble talent for diplomacy and an intuitive skill for cultivating the right friendships.

Savile went on to gain a degree in Classics at Balliol College, Oxford, and when he left university in 1880 he returned to Somerleyton. He had come of age by then and was taking control of the estate, buying more land and hiring more staff inside and outside the hall. Not surprisingly, the running costs of Somerleyton escalated from around £6,000 a year to over £50,000.

Savile (far left) at College, 1879 in the Balliol Four rowing team

Sir Savile sprinkled money liberally around the region with donations to every conceivable charity, society and sporting association. Entries in his personal accounts for the coming years would include sums for the Lowestoft Sailors' Home, the Fire Brigade, the Wherrymen's Mission, the Asylum for Idiots, and Gorleston Cottage Hospital, as well as amounts for various flower shows, sewing schemes, rifle clubs and even the Lowestoft Homing Pigeon Society.

As patron of the local school and church, he had further outgoings to cover. The estate was bringing in increasing sums with better management of the farms and marshland, and Sir Savile's shares in the Crossley Carpet empire provided a comfortable income. He could not afford to maintain family grudges though, and he began to play an active part in the company's dealings. Eventually he would take over as chairman.

Never highlighted as a great scholar but with a good head for business and an articulate tongue, Sir Savile would soon prove the old adage that it isn't necessarily what you know, but who you know, that counts most. Now he could include the Prince of Wales among his acquaintances and Edward visited Somerleyton on at least one occasion, when no expense was spared in an effort to impress the future king.

Sir Savile's reputation as a generous host and benefactor boosted his popularity among all classes and that stood him in good stead when the time came for him to offer himself as a political candidate. He became Liberal MP for Lowestoft and North Suffolk in 1885. With typical enthusiasm he dived into the political whirlpool and caused some large ripples. Adamant in his opposition to Gladstone's Home Rule Bill for Ireland, he took the shocking step of voting against his own party and in 1886 he took his voters with him to the Liberal Unionist Party.

Sir Savile was leading a very active life, yet still it could be enhanced if he had someone to share it all with and he had become most eligible in the eyes of son-in-law seekers. It would take a beautiful, amusing and well-connected young woman to secure the hand of this dynamic bachelor, and it was inevitable that he would set his sights on just such a lady. He was now dividing his time between London, Halifax and Somerleyton like his father before him, but his business interests also included dealings in Market Harborough in Leicestershire and he hunted regularly in the county. A fellow huntsman in that fashionable set was Harry Lawson, later Lord Burnham the owner of the Daily Telegraph, who had married into a most colourful family by the name of de Bathe. Soon they would become Sir Savile's in-laws too.

The de Bathe lineage could be traced back to the Norman Conquests and their ancestors had been given great manors, particularly in Ireland. The latest in line, Sir Henry de Bathe, was a dapper devil-may-care sort who had started out in life with every advantage. Described as one of the most handsome and popular officers in the Brigade of Guards, he had wealth, social status, and all the right connections. However, his charming manners could be turned on and off, he was known to be sarcastic and impatient of those he considered fools, including many of his army superiors, and grudges quickly formed in high places so that any hope of a dazzling military career was smothered. Henry seemed not to care a fig, he was too busy enjoying himself. His hedonistic approach to life had made him welcome among the leading actors, artists, wits and authors of the 1840's, and this had led him to fall in love with a dancer, Miss Charlotte Clare. His father had forbidden them to marry and threatened disinheritance so Henry's response had been to live with her anyway. A large family of illegitimate children followed, the last of them being a daughter, Phyllis, born in 1869. A year later her grandfather died, leaving her parents free to marry and produce two more children, including the next heir, Hugo.

Phyllis de Bathe grew into a tall and elegant beauty with golden hair and large, limpid eyes. With a beguiling lisp and a tinkling laugh, Phyllis loved a joke more than anything and she was perfectly at ease in any company. A

General Sir Henry de Bathe KCB

favourite of the Prince of Wales himself, she was the toast of London Society - they nicknamed her 'The Lily' and a cluster of ardent admirers gathered wherever she went. Sir Savile Crossley was among them and he quickly made up his mind to have her for his own. Phyllis found his quiet confidence and boyish good looks to her liking and their growing attachment was noted as they shared carriage rides and trips to the races. An engagement was announced.

The match meant the Crossleys' vast fortune would be combined with the status of an ancient pedigree, although Phyllis' family was a somewhat infamous one. It was just the sort of event that the wagging tongues of Society loved.

The wedding date was set for 14 December 1887, by which time Phyllis

Phyllis, 'The Lily'

was aged 18 and her fiancé 30. The Lowestoft Journal reported, 'In spite of terrible weather no ceremony could possibly have been brighter than the wedding of Sir Savile Crossley MP and Miss Phyllis de Bathe at St Peter's, Eaton Square. Sir Henry looked stalwart in a coat adorned with brass buttons and his youngest daughter in her becoming dress of white duchesse satin and old Brussels lace, was unanimously pronounced to be the most beautiful bride of the Jubilee year. The bridesmaids were arrayed in tan-coloured cloth, faille français silver embroidery and draperies lined with pale coral silk. Their initial diamond brooches and large bouquets of dark chrysanthemums were gifts of the bridegroom.'

The guest list was studded with the names of lords and ladies, and politicians of all shades were present. The report continued, 'Nearly the whole of the guests afterwards migrated in the rain to the Buckingham Palace Hotel, where Lady de Bathe received at afternoon tea and everyone looked respectfully at the priceless diamonds, pearls and sapphires worth over £40,000 as well as the Prince of Wales's golden bangle, until the time came for Lady Crossley to depart for Paris, in a dainty travelling dress of shot-plush in shades of opal, with Amazon cloth to match, and trimmings of steel and silver embroidery.'

Well might the guests drool over the glittering array of wedding presents. Sir Savile had given his bride a treasure trove of diamond-encrusted jewellery, and in total Phyllis received more than a dozen diamond bracelets from friends and family, along with a galaxy of other sparkling baubles including the bejewelled bangle from the Prince of Wales. The more prosaic guests had donated mainly silverware, such as fruit bowls, salvers and trays for calling cards. Later a Society report of Phyllis' appearance at a VIP ball would show that she derived much pleasure from gilding her lily-white arms and throat. It enthused, 'Her great beauty was set off by a unique display of diamonds. Diamond bracelets reached from her wrists almost to her shoulders and she also wore numerous diamond necklaces.'

Back at Somerleyton, the tenants and employees were relishing their share of the bridegroom's generosity on his wedding day. From noon until dusk the church bells rang out at intervals, and flags flew from many houses while bunting fluttered along the length of the drive to the hall. First a group of almost 100 estate men came up for refreshments and to toast the happy couple. Next around 300 children from Somerleyton and the adjoining villages came for a tea party of undreamed-of proportions. They were seated at tables under the massive glass roof of the winter garden, the glow on the children's faces reflecting the warm light thrown out by the gas jets in the dome above the fountain, where rainbows danced in the spray of water from the mouths of stone dolphins. While the brass band played, the estate agent Kerry Rix threw himself into the fray and helped keep the massed ranks of exuberant children fed and occupied. Afterwards they were treated to a magic lantern show in the dining room, before being packed off home with another share of goodies and gifts.

Finally the gardeners, stable men and house servants took to the floor of the dining hall for a dance, followed by supper at ten o'clock when food and wine flowed freely and toasts were drunk with great gusto. The dance continued until well into the night, or for as long as the 50 or so guests could still be found standing.

Two weeks after the wedding, Sir Savile and Lady Crossley hosted a grand banquet for the Mayor and Corporation of Lowestoft at Somerleyton Hall. In contrast they then provided a New Year's treat for the inmates of Oulton Workhouse, sending a feast of meats, tarts, puddings and 241 mince pies direct from the hall kitchen. With the agent Kerry Rix and Charles Howes their butler the couple circulated among the residents and encouraged them to join in the celebration of the recent happy event. A local press reporter was there too and wrote, 'As the eye roamed over the different classes assembled, we were struck with the variety of characters, and could only feel there was before us a kind of microcosm of society, only in its more painful features. We had pointed out to us, for instance, a once fine-looking specimen of humanity in the person of a decayed barrister at law, another a former superintendent of the railway service, a third, a once flourishing farmer, also a doctor and a minister.' Later, slides were shown to the inmates that depicted the grand residence of Sir Savile and Lady Crossley, as well as other views of the magnificent estate that was theirs.

Phyllis did not dwell on the great gulf that divided the fabulously rich

Phyllis and Savile (top and bottom, left)with friends

from the woefully poor. In her stately bridal home she was happy to while away some free time copying out love poems, ordering the finest new gowns to be worn only once and smoking special Turkish cigarettes that cost more than a working man's weekly wage. But in the coming years she would find that her bed was not filled with roses and money did not grow on trees.

The year after the wedding, Dame Martha released her interest in the Halifax property Belle Vue and signed it over to her son. By now it had been virtually unused for a decade, and a local writer had declared that 'both Lady Crossley and her son Sir Savile have by their prolonged absence indicated that they have no liking for the residence.' Sir Savile did eventually sell Belle Vue to the Halifax Corporation, but his links with the town were far from severed. He would continue to help charities there, and would become their MP, finally being made a Freeman of the Borough in recognition of his loyalty.

Meanwhile, with a new Lady Crossley on the scene at Somerleyton Hall, Martha decided to move out. It was not as if the newlyweds needed the extra space, but she had little in common with her daughter-in-law anyway, and had no desire to play gooseberry. She felt especially out of place when the fun-loving de Bathe family came to call in their droves, and would not see herself retreating to a wing of her own home.

First Martha moved to Kirkley, which was then a parish adjoining

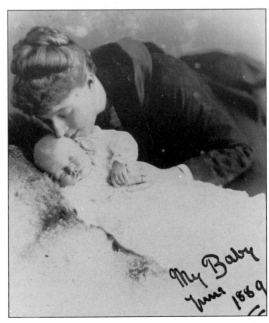

Martha's first grandson with his mother Phyllis

Lowestoft. Her final home was Flixton House, just a few miles away from her son, and in 1889 she had the pleasure of seeing a new Somerleyton heir brought home, a grandson named Francis Savile after the two men who had been dearest to her. Her first granddaughter, christened Phyllis, was born just 10 months later.

Now Martha spent much of her time at home with her companion Miss Evans, or writing letters with the help of a young neighbour, Miss Cubitt. She enjoyed being driven around the neighbourhood by her coachman but her health was failing rapidly and in her last few years she could barely move from her room. Early in August 1891 Sir Savile was on a yachting cruise off the coast of Norway, taking Phyllis there in an effort to alleviate her own health problems. He was summoned home urgently with the news that his mother had taken very ill indeed. For two weeks the tough 70-year-old fought the inevitable before slipping quietly into eternal rest. Describing her as an 'amiable lady' with a 'gentle disposition', local reports told of the great gloom that settled on the district with the passing of Lady Martha Crossley.

The late dowager had forbidden her family to indulge in the Victorian desire for lavish expressions of grief - there was to be as little pomp or ritual as possible. Sir Savile followed the open hearse on foot so that the many tenants and employees who came to pay their respects could join the procession. It took nearly an hour to reach Somerleyton Church, where there was to be hardly any time for weeping and wailing. Martha had decreed that there would be no hymns sung and no Death March played. The whole service lasted just 20 minutes from entering the solemn church to laying the last wreath at the graveside. Martha's remains were laid in a large brick grave lined with moss and white flowers. Her close family were reported to have struggled to control their emotions, but expressed their profound grief in floral tributes. There were restrained tokens of respect from the Halifax Crossleys.

And so Lady Martha Eliza Crossley ended her lifetime of direct, sometimes confrontational action, driven by firm principles. She had risen through the ranks of financial comfort and social respectability, and seen her son married into nobility. Even so, her final wish speaks volumes about her attitude towards the vast business empire that had made her such a wealthy woman. She had asked that her husband Sir Francis' remains should be removed from their resting place at Halifax and laid by her side in Somerleyton. Her last request was denied.

Martha's possessions were valued at £41,010 and after several legacies she bequeathed most of her personal effects to Sir Savile. They added a few drops to his ocean of wealth, but Dame Martha's most precious legacy to her son would be her contribution to his character, one which attracted for him a lifetime of praise, recognition and achievement.

Sir Savile continued to take on high-profile roles. No longer standing for parliament he served as a Justice of the Peace, a Deputy Lieutenant for Suffolk and in 1896 he was High Sheriff for Suffolk. He took a keen interest in local hospital charities and that, combined with his close friendship with the Prince of Wales, led him to devote a great deal of energy to helping set up a new organisation which sought to bring some order to the confusion of charity-run hospitals in London.

By 1891 there had been a burgeoning of hospitals in the city, many set up under the Poor Laws to treat infectious diseases, but nearly 400 more were financed by charities, and were managed with varying levels of competence. There was rivalry, overlapping of services, and a growing unease among subscribers that the whole business of hospital provision would soon have to be taken over by the State, ending their independence. Of course, the middle classes could pay their way if they needed nursing care, but philanthropists like Sir Savile wanted to see that poorer people had the chance of a good, well-run hospital service too, as long as there was no hint of socialism involved. The Prince of Wales was already supporting dozens of London hospitals, and as Queen Victoria's diamond jubilee year approached, he agreed to harness the goodwill of the people and instigate a massive collection of money to create a central body which could oversee the voluntary hospitals and make substantial grants if they merited it.

A committee was appointed and Sir Savile Crossley was among the handpicked team of ten men, which was headed by Lord Rothschild. Under the weighty banner of The Prince of Wales's Hospital Fund for London to Commemorate the Sixtieth Year of the Queen's Reign, they set up an office at the Bank of England and went out to raise their target of £1 million in capital, and an annual income of over £100,000. In his history of the Fund, entitled Philanthropy and the Hospitals of London, Frank Prochaska wrote, 'In a charity so dependant on the active support of the royal family, an important initial appointment was Sir Savile Crossley (later Lord Somerleyton) as an Honorary Secretary. He was the first in a line of unpaid staff for whom the institution became a way of life. For over thirty years he provided a crucial link between the Fund and its royal presidents...He was known at court for his shooting and his diplomatic skills. In the Fund, the former were an advantage, the latter indispensable.'

Frank Prochaska points out that the Fund had few Liberal politicians on its books, and here again Sir Savile's contacts and skills would prove invaluable in the coming years. From the start the institution was cheap to run, which, says Prochaska, 'would not have been possible without the unpaid and unflagging services of the Honorary Secretaries and Committee men. Crossley, who contributed £500 to the Fund each year, took work home with him when he returned to his estate in Suffolk, an unusual practice for a Victorian country gentleman.'

Sir Savile was no ordinary country gentleman. Even with his tailored suits and top-drawer associates, he owed much of his character to his northern roots. He cared deeply about the poorer classes and he could not settle in with the carefree, frivolous society so beloved by his wife. Their daughter Monica gave a clue to his real interests when she described a typical Sunday afternoon in London. 'After lunch, it was usually Tattersalls with Dad, or the zoo. I remember once Dad took us to St Paul's on top of a horse-bus - that was a great event. I don't remember St Paul's much, but the bus ride is vivid in my mind, with Dad moving further and further forward until he could sit and talk horses with the driver.' At home in Suffolk, Savile would take his daughters to visit their neighbours, and when one farmer's wife proudly boasted that her daughter could play the piano, he retorted, 'Well, mine can milk a cow'. It was true, he had been determined that his eldest daughter Phyllis, nicknamed Noons, should acquire the skill.

Pretension was anathema to him, and sometimes he needed to get away from the whole Society scene. When in London Sir Savile's retreat was his Club, Brooks's, but in Suffolk he had the whole countryside to lose himself in. For a short time at least he could walk, ride, shoot and fish without interruption or demand, if he wished. Fortunately he was blessed with a strong constitution, in contrast to Phyllis, whose pale beauty seemed to go hand-in-hand with very delicate health. Her personal scrapbook contains many news cuttings about her absences from the social scene. For instance, it was reported, 'Pretty Lady Crossley is very unwell, and will enjoy no more gaieties this Season. It seems to be the old story of 'doing too much', but her fair face will be greatly missed this year, especially by those who are indebted to her for so much enjoyment at her dance'.

However, she collected many mementoes of events that she had managed to attend, particularly shooting parties at various country estates, and race meetings. Indeed, her devotion to the latter seems to have sometimes had a direct bearing on her health. One of her younger relatives recalled, 'Auntie Phyl was very formidable, she had a biting wit. As a small girl I was terrified of her! She was tall and rather made up, her passion in life was racing and betting. Uncle Savile was very small with a quiet sense of humour. When Auntie Phyl's racing debts had grown enormous she would say "Oh! Savile Darling, I feel so ill, I don't know what's wrong with me." When her husband had become sufficiently anxious, she just mentioned the trifling sums that she owed the bookmakers - he always paid up.'

Sir Savile's own idea of a cure for his wife's ills often involved trips abroad, but on one occasion that in itself proved quite stressful. A newspaper reported, 'Beautiful Lady Crossley has come back from her yachting cruise, much benefited in health. Sir Savile hired the steam yacht Giralda, of three hundred tons, and carried his wife off to the calm beauties of the Norwegian fjords. The adventurous folk started in a gale, and for three days and nights endured unutterable tossings, with the usual heartrending accompaniments.' Although the weather improved, the trip was further marred when a man from a nearby boat drowned, in spite of heroic efforts by Sir Savile, who dived in to try and save him. The baronet had a courageous spirit in many ways, and the Victorian rage for adventure and hunting did not escape him. He was a keen collector of big game trophies and one journalist, in describing Somerleyton Hall, commented, 'I venture to think no house contains a collection of trophies of the chase finer than that at Somerleyton Hall.' There were, it noted, mounted beasts from the Rockies, Algeria, Spain, Egypt, Norway and other countries. In pride of place were two stuffed polar bears rampant, which Sir Savile himself had brought back from the island of Spitzbergen in 1897.

That expedition attracted much admiration and many requests for him to recount his exploits, with lantern slides showing snatches of the action. He called his lecture 'a trip to the edge of the ice' and Sir Savile usually introduced the entertainment with modesty, saying, 'Please understand that it is only a record of a month's trip by a tourist under the most advantageous circumstances possible.' He told of the journey North with his friend and guide Mr Arnold Pike in a small ship, a steam-driven sealer, and how the pair had to wait two days for their Norwegian crew to get sober before they could settle down to the business of the kill. Sir Savile added 'They were all to a man teetotallers after we started, for there was no liquor on board except for emergencies.'

When the bloodshed began walrus, seal and bear were taken in large numbers, valued for their fat as much as for their skins and of the 57 polar bears that the hunters tracked down, only two were brought back alive. The remainder made their way to the taxidermists, and were destined finally to rest in peace in front of fashionable hearths or to stand frozen for decades in attitudes of belated defiance.

One cannot help but moot the question of whether it was brave, cruel or just plain crazy for the men to pit themselves against nature, when reading again Sir Savile's description of the hunt. 'The general method of shooting bears is to stalk them', he recounted, 'but they may be found in round beds they make in the snow or may be decoyed by a man lying on his back and waving his legs in the air, in which case they come slowly at first but with a final rush on what they imagine to be their prey.'

Phyllis' attention was now focused on a new arrival, their fourth child Monica. A son christened John had been born in 1893 and the family was complete. Their final baby, William, would be born in November 1903 and would survive for only three weeks. Lady Crossley's health remained indifferent but a team of maids, nannies, nurses and governesses took charge of the children and her strength improved once more, allowing her to reassume her title as one of Society's most successful hostesses. Some events simply could not be missed. Prince Edward paid a visit to Somerleyton in 1899 and the following year he was entertained at the Crossleys' London home in Carlton House Terrace.

Prince Edward at Somerleyton with Phyllis (front) and Savile standing behind the Prince.

Edward declined to sign the visitors' book.

When the Season was over, Phyllis' larger-than-life relatives were frequent visitors to Somerleyton and one former member of staff had the feeling that in Sir Savile's eyes, they sometimes outstayed their welcome. Their eccentricities are part of the family legend, and topping the list for notoriety beyond the call of duty is her brother Hugo, the de Bathe heir who was nicknamed Shuggie.

In 1897 Shuggie was following his father's example of partying with

Phyllis and Shuggie

the glitterati rather than carving out a noble career, and at a function hosted by the Duke of Richmond he met the Prince of Wales' mistress, Lillie Langtry. Apparently with Bertie's blessing and even encouragement they formed a relationship, even though he was almost 20 years her junior. In 1899 they married. Almost immediately they went their separate ways and gave no impression of being a devoted couple. On the contrary, many said that a deal had been struck so that Lillie could achieve her ambition of becoming a real Lady. To her chagrin, Sir Henry de Bathe showed no intention of relinquishing his title by dying, and he banned his new daughter-in-law from his house. He did have a photograph of her though - he wrote 'Jezebel' on it and hung it in the lavatory.

In later years she became less welcome at Phyllis' house too. One former parlour maid recalled 'I opened the door to Lillie Langtry when Hugo de Bathe returned very ill from Madrid. He didn't see her, as her Ladyship told me to say he was not at home. Well, I was a young cockney, 15 years old, so I told the Jersey Lily to hop it!' This was not the kind of treatment Lillie was accustomed to, but even she knew better than to argue against her sister-in-law Phyllis.

Some say that Lillie tried to use her influence to keep Shuggie safe during the Boer War, possibly to protect her own future title, others insist that she was glad to see him go, and he glad to leave. Nevertheless he departed to fight the Boers and came through it alive to help her achieve her ambition when Sir Henry died in 1907.

At Somerleyton, Sir Savile's impending service caused genuine demonstrations of admiration and goodwill. Before he left, he arranged for Phyllis to assume power of attorney over the entire estate, with free rein to buy property, attend to the management of their land, pay bills, and enter into any contracts she saw fit. Undeniably, she had the benefit of the best advisors and, along with Kerry Rix the agent, the most experienced stewards and staff, but this demonstration of trust showed a marked change of attitude from the days when Martha was left as virtually a tenant of her own home.

Lady Crossley would do more than keep Somerleyton Hall and Estate ticking over in the absence of her husband. She would actively promote his career, putting him back into the political spotlight and helping him to reach the pinnacle of his public service.

Chapter 2

Mixed Feelings and Fortunes

———————∽∾———————

While Savile was away there was a general election, popularly labelled the 'Khaki Election' because it was seen to be making the most of the country's surge of patriotism. Phyllis waged a hard-hitting campaign in his absence and he was elected as the new Conservative MP for Halifax, his late father's old constituency. In May 1901 he took parliamentary leave from the Boer War and, to his great embarrassment, there was a hero's welcome awaiting him at Somerleyton. As he stepped down from the train there were gun salutes, foghorns, trumpets and cheers from the crowd and all along the route home the roads were crammed with more people waving flags and craning their necks for a glimpse of him. The gardeners had put up two great floral arches, the first bearing the family motto 'Omne Bonum ab Alto' - 'Everything Good is from Above' and the second said simply, 'Welcome Home'. At the hall gates the procession stopped and a team of hefty men replaced the horses, hauling their master's carriage along the last half mile to the festooned courtyard of Somerleyton Hall.

Speeches and songs, tributes and applause followed and there was a lengthy address in appreciation for Savile's efforts both in the war and at home. Standing self-consciously with one hand thrust deep in his pocket, he thanked them and added, 'As matters stand at present I shall probably have to leave England as soon as the House rises in August to have another turn after the Boers.' In fact the war ended without Sir Savile having to return to South

Africa, but his actions had meant promotion to Lieutenant Colonel of the 71st Company (Sharpshooters) of the Imperial Yeomanry.

A hero's welcome - Sir Savile's return from the Boer War, 1901

As soon as he was ensconced back in Somerleyton he took charge of the estate once more and found it virtually unchanged. Most of the old faces were still there and Sir Savile wanted to show that he was the same man too, not a hero to be worshipped from afar. At the first opportunity he slipped back into his comfy old clothes and went riding on the estate, or launched an attack on the flowerbeds and borders, searching out weeds and tending his precious rhododendrons.

At the hall he called in his agent to show him the books, picking over them carefully and questioning any possible anomaly. He found it all in perfect order; the accounts had been kept meticulously up to date by Kerry Rix and his clerk, detailing every penny that was spent and showing every source of income too. There were the cottage and allotment rents, the sale of farm produce such as butter, wool, skins and livestock, the sale of timber from the woods, and there was Sir Savile's income from his Crossley shares. On the payments side Kerry had noted down all the running costs of the estate including the wages of the hall staff and the gardeners, engineers, painters, joiners, bricklayers, and woodsmen.

There were other costs for leisure and pleasure as well as costs for simply keeping up appearances. Bills had come in from hairdressers, tailors and shoemakers; one entry records 19 shillings paid for a cricket bat; 8s.6d. for a footwarmer, and various amounts for wines and spirits. For outdoor pursuits, valuable horses for every course gleamed in the stables, and alongside the coaches there too was Savile's latest acquisition, a Brooke motor car, fresh from the Lowestoft manufacturer.

In the warm summer that followed he would draw a cautious crowd whenever he took to the road. At that time the motor car was purely a luxury item as opposed to a practical means of transport. At the speed limit of 14 miles per hour, raised to 20 in 1903, it would have taken Sir Savile days to reach London and probably weeks to get to Halifax. Phyllis must have been in two minds about the safety of the new vehicle - she would not even travel in a hansom cab when they were in London because she considered them to be dangerous. She liked comfort and those early cars were not noted for it. She liked to look her best, but silk gowns and elaborate hairstyles were not compatible with the rough rides experienced by many pioneer passengers. Mostly the family walked whenever they could, or they took to their trusty four-wheeled carriage. When they went to London for the Season their horses, carriages and coachmen travelled with them on the train. In time, the excitement and scene-stealing popularity of the motor car would appeal to that side of Phyllis' character that craved attention. Meanwhile it was a rare occurrence for villagers to see a car chugging along the dusty, rutted roads around Somerleyton.

A carriage awaits at Somerleyton

Sir Savile was not the first car-owner in the district. Local man Sam Cole wrote of this boyhood memory, 'I well remember the first motor car to arrive in the village. A notice was sent to the schoolmaster that the car was coming and we were lined up in the road, to see what a wonderful thing it was. I suppose it was travelling about five miles an hour or less because a man was walking in front with a red flag. We all thought this was wonderful but we felt sorry for the man who had to walk with the flag. As time went on, cars were improved and his Lordship bought one and the red flag was done away with. I well remember my father coming home late for tea one day and telling us what a wonderful experience he had had. He was taken for a ride in the new motor car. He said it was a wonderful feeling to sit there with the thing gathering speed and nothing in front to pull it. "I would not have missed that ride for anything" he said.'

Not all the villagers approved; Vic Houghton's grandfather lived to over 100 and, says Vic, 'He used to come out for walks near the school. I remember we saw a local doctor who'd just got a motor car, which was unusual in those days you see, and he saw that coming along, he said, "'Pend on it - we didn't have those things when I was a boy". 'Cause he was a horseman, you see. If you're a horseman, you're jealous of motor cars taking over.'

There was more to it than just resistance to change. At first, every time a wheezing, chuffing car came by, riders and cart drivers had to dismount and hold their horse's bridle, trying their best to soothe the terrified animal as it reared and plunged to get away from the mechanical monster. Many a horseman would shake his fist and curse the new contraption that could so upset both his horse and cart. Such dissenters whose faith in horses remained firm would see justice brought to bear. The rough roads took their toll mercilessly on the fragile vehicles and Kerry Rix recorded many entries for 'motor repairs' in his ledgers. The blame might not have been entirely due to the road conditions. According to his daughter Monica, Sir Savile himself never did manage to get the hang of driving.

Savile's taste for good living continued. He still enjoyed visiting friends, race-going, hunting and shooting, but there was evidence of a subtle change in him, possibly as a result of his experiences at war. Despite making light of the hardships he had endured, he mentioned on several occasions his regret that a man who had served him for seven years and had enlisted alongside him, had been seized with enteric fever when they arrived back at Southampton. The disease had been rife in South Africa and the doctors knew little about it. He warned others to be careful about their health and to see a doctor at once if they were unwell. At the same time he recognised that proper medical care was just too expensive for many people and he threw himself into his work at the London hospital fund he had helped to set up for Prince Edward.

With the death of Queen Victoria, the committee had taken the opportunity to launch a Coronation appeal and from January 1902 the organisation was re-named King Edward's Hospital Fund for London. Thanks to a much-publicised campaign in which Savile played a major role, there was a huge injection of cash into the Fund's coffers. He continued to donate large sums to a number of charities and he worked tirelessly for hospitals in Suffolk as well as in the city. The time would come when his generosity would help bring him within sight of financial ruin.

For now, he resolved that loyalty should have its just reward for his staff and their dependants. He could afford to give a helping hand to those in need and in the following years he maintained a patrician regime, whereby the villagers on his Somerleyton estate could expect compassion and security, provided they toed the line. Sir Savile had always been acknowledged as a shrewd squire. He was among the first to provide allotments for his labourers, not only so they could supplement their income with home-grown produce but also to give them a stake in the land and perhaps stem the tide of workers who at the turn of the century were rushing towards the towns. Now though, he occasionally set aside business acumen in favour of philanthropy.

In one instance he set up a workshop where coir mats were woven, but for years the venture made a loss. The only clue as to why the deficit was allowed to continue is shown in the accounts, where the weaver, on a wage of 7s.6d. a week, is stated to be William Smith. The worker's identity is further revealed in a poem by Tommy Crawford about the village at the turn of the century:

> 'Down Floral Loke then you would find
> the only villager of his kind;
> Blind Billy was as blind as bats,
> would sit all day there making mats'.

Savile was fulfilling his parents' vow to help the needy not just with charity, but with employment. Later he would give war veterans priority for farm tenancies and the accounts indicate that several widows enjoyed rent-free accommodation, whereas in other circumstances and with a different landlord their fate would most likely have been the workhouse. Another young man who fraudulently cashed a cheque from Sir Savile was given a second chance, provided he mended his ways.

Sir Savile did not have more money than sense though. He waged a bitter battle against the local water board over compensation for a new scheme that affected his land. He could call on the best brains for advice and he pulled strings to protect his interests, but when he later sold his London house, his obstinacy in ignoring professional advice gained him a much better price than his agents anticipated. He was frequently away from Somerleyton on business and delegated power to Kerry Rix, his right-hand man. As agent, he represented his employer and was overseer of all the outside workers who in turn had their own hierarchy, in which those at the top ruled their territory as diligently as if the land and buildings were their own. They respected their squire and in turn Savile never failed to doff his hat in greeting to them or stop to enquire after their family.

Sir Savile's own children adored him and clamoured for his favour, demanding piggybacks and games whenever they spent time alone with him. His friends admired him and among them Bertie, now King Edward Vll, relied upon him a great deal. For the first few years of the new century it seemed as if life could hardly be better for the Somerleyton Crossleys.

Phyllis was certainly enjoying the Good Life. She had shaken off her youthful romanticism and had emerged with a sharp tongue and an expensive taste for being at the cutting edge of fashion. She had made a name as a stunning vision of expensive couture, she smoked, gambled and made fun of people, but none of these were seen as vices among her circle of smart friends. At Somerleyton she missed the Society spotlight and disliked the damp winds that blew in from the North Sea. She had no time for chit-chat with the staff, and even guests needed to be wary of showing chinks in their emotional armour. One friend of Sir Savile's is reported as having exclaimed, 'Madam, I may be a worm, but I am a guest worm!'

Phyllis' granddaughter Mary adds, 'She was a very beautiful, very made-up, very tall and imposing Edwardian type lady and she was also very critical. Granny was tremendously funny, but always at other people's expense. I can remember her personal maid, who seemed dreadfully old to me. She probably wasn't very old at all, but she was small and she used to creep round Granny, and I can remember Granny saying to her "Of all the classes in the world, there's no such impossible class as the servant class." And her maid would say "Yes M'Lady, quite agree, M'Lady." She stayed a long time, so there must have been some kind of bond, but Granny was incredibly rude to staff, always. They weren't allowed in the front of the house once the family were up and about, and the rest of the time they were expected to be seen and not heard. But they all seemed to adore her, for some reason.'

Lady Crossley was simply a woman of her time, in an age when servants had little status or consideration. Because her attitude was the norm, the servants themselves thought little of it and those who did feel aggrieved had to find another occupation. Most of the Somerleyton staff would have remained anonymous to this day had it not been for the changing attitude of the next Crossley generation.

The four children of Sir Savile and Phyllis were growing up in an environment of splendour and stimulation but with few opportunities for making their own friends. The girls never went to school. As was the custom, Monica and her elder sister Phyllis, who was always nicknamed 'Noons', were taught by a governess at home until they were sixteen, when they were sent abroad to Finishing School. They could not mix with the village children and they rarely went to parties, which usually involved a long journey, although Monica was allowed to play with the Rector's daughter Jill Bean, who was six years her junior.

Monica made up for her loneliness by spending many a happy hour hovering in the company of her parents' employees. Whenever she was free from her long-suffering governess named Miss Roberts, she would roam the hall and gardens in search of adventure. In her memoirs she recorded her impressions of some well remembered characters and their activities: people like Charles Howes the butler, Garner, who was valet to her father, and Lily Giles the head housemaid until Emma Jaggard took over.

She continued, 'Jimmy Cole, after many years as Team Man at Kitty Farm, was brought into the garden to help with sweeping up etc. He made no complaint, but when I asked him how he liked it, he replied rather sadly, "Oh, that's alright, you know. But I did love my farm". Sam Saker was Farm Bailiff and the best looking man I ever saw. He would have been a very suitable model for a picture of Our Lord. As his wife used to say, "My husband, he ain't no scholar". There was TB on both sides of the family, all the children died and Sam was left alone. My dad put him into a cottage close by Fritton Lake, with a few hens to give him an interest, and he got two elderly women to look after him. He was never known to complain.'

'On the estate, Hurley was the electrician, with only one eye. He and his wife, who was rather a friend of mine, lived in the picturesque little 'Back Lodge', on one floor with reed thatch and a gay little garden. Old Balls was another of my friends. He was the estate painter, who was expected to die quite young, and always looked delicate and spoke in a quavering voice. Emma Cory was head laundry maid for over 21 years, doing superb work, with two others under her. Emma was a good friend of my Nanny Hilditch, and so of mine.'

'When my father pulled down the winter garden in 1914, Frank Smith who had worked there for years doing all the stoking of fires, watering and tending the thousands of pot plants, moved into the house and became boot black and coal and wood carrier and 'valet' to my brothers. He also walked the letters across the deer park to the Post Office every afternoon.'

Monica concluded 'These were just some of my father's enormous household, most of whom were truly dear to us.' Later she would talk about the village characters whom she and her sister Noons visited, such as Laura Oldman who was confined to bed but from the window of her Widow's Cottage she could see the village life going on below. There were several other elderly or disabled people who would stand at certain street corners, hoping to meet someone willing to stop for a chat. The two main meeting places became known as Crock's Corners, and Phyllis had seats put there to make their wait more comfortable. When she herself was aged over 80, Monica would say, 'I still remember all their names, and those of the many servants in the house, and workmen on the estate. They all left an impression that never fades. How surprised they'd be to know how much they mattered to us.'

Monica's older brother Frank, the Somerleyton heir, was dispatched to boarding school from the age of eight, but when home on holiday he had much more freedom than the girls did. His particular friend was Sam Cole, the son of the farm bailiff. Sam recalled, 'During his holidays from Eton he would spend most of his time at the farm with me. Often he would be at the farm at 5 am, rattling a stick on our bedroom window for me to go out for a swim in the lake. On our return we would call home and Mother would make us a cup of tea. Mother was never very happy when we were out playing, she was so afraid something might happen and I might get the blame for it. She was very frightened because sometimes we would quarrel and fight. I was always afraid to hit him as hard as he hit me, as the marks would show and I would get into trouble. I think Mother was very glad when we all went back to school.'

Sam's father died in 1901 following an accident on the farm. A first-rate horseman, he was kicked by a young colt during its training. His wounded leg failed to heal and was amputated but he did not recover. Sam said, 'Mother gave us his last message; he said, "bid my little children goodbye and tell them I have gone to be with Jesus."' Those little children would have to grow up very quickly if they were to stay one step ahead of the hunger and deprivation that often befell the fatherless. New laws meant that the tragic event had to be fully investigated and after the inquest, Mrs Cole received £200 compensation from Sir Savile. She received a pension of 3s.6d. a week and a cottage was provided for them rent-free. Sam also earned 3s.6d. a week by working long, hard hours on the farm. He was waiting for a vacancy in the hall gardens and when that did arise, he helped occasionally in the house itself. Many years later he would become butler there.

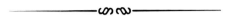

Following his distinguished service in the Boer War, Sir Savile's career moved up in leaps and bounds. In 1902 the Duke of Marlborough resigned from the office of Paymaster General and Prime Minister Balfour recommended Sir Savile Crossley for the post, describing him as 'a man of character and decision', and 'generally popular.' The King agreed. It was a great honour for Savile to be appointed as overseer of payments for the work of the Civil Service and Government Departments. In the same year he was created Member of the Royal Victorian Order (MVO) and a Privy Councillor. In August he was thrown from his horse and broke his collarbone, but he was never the type to let such trivial annoyances stop him working. In 1905 he became chairman of the Crossley carpet empire, requiring trips to Halifax for the monthly board meetings. He missed very few of them.

The next General Election of 1906 saw the Conservatives routed and Sir Savile, standing as a Liberal Unionist, lost his Halifax seat. He relinquished his title of Paymaster General too. However there was no let-up in the Crossleys' activities, political or personal. In June 1906 a London Society report effused, 'Quite one of the smartest gatherings will be Lady Crossley's dance in Carlton House Terrace, and this week too the Prince and Princess of Wales are honouring Sir Savile and Lady Crossley by dining with them. Lady Crossley is an admirable hostess, who not only looks very handsome and is always beautifully dressed, but has the art of getting just the right people together.'

There was entertaining on a grand scale at Somerleyton too. In August 1907 a local newspaper reported the third annual excursion to Somerleyton Hall by members of the Halifax Conservative Union. A massive party of 1,700 people came from Yarmouth to Somerleyton by river in chartered pleasure steamers, and then a convoy of wagonettes carried them to the Park gates, leaving them to stroll along the drive to the hall terrace. The report continued, 'Here Sir Savile and Lady Crossley received their guests, shaking hands with each member of the party. Many of the men were accompanied by their wives and children, and others by their sweethearts. The procession seemed an almost interminable one, but the hosts maintained their position until everyone had been received.' The guests took refreshment in the winter garden and then wandered at will around the immaculate lawns and flowerbeds outside, while music was provided by the band of the Prince of Wales Own Norfolk Artillery, of which Sir Savile was an honorary Lieutenant Colonel. Even the weather, the only aspect over which the host had no control, was perfect.

At that time the Liberal Party held a majority in parliament and Sir Savile's influence in that quarter was called upon when the King Edward VII Hospital Fund needed to pass a bill to reform their constitution. His skill as a diplomat won the day and his efforts were much appreciated in the highest circles. In 1909 Sir Savile became a Knight Commander of the Royal Victorian Order, a KCVO in recognition of his services to the King.

The tragedy of Edward VII's death in May 1910 was sorely felt at Somerleyton Hall and a great gloom settled temporarily on the house. In the same year Sir Savile was again thwarted in his effort to become an MP, this time standing for West Islington, London. Lady Crossley had put a great deal of effort into supporting him, telling one gathering of ladies, 'I have known the candidate intimately for 22 years; in fact, I think I may claim him as my oldest and best friend; and putting my personal interest entirely on one side I will say this, that although he and I have not always seen eye to eye, or been entirely in accord, our differences of opinion have in no way altered our friendship. If you want a man for integrity, if you want a man to work for your interests, if you are looking for a hard-working man to represent this borough, I have no hesitation in recommending my old friend, your prospective candidate.'

This curious reference to their increasingly public disagreements did not help to convince the voters and Sir Savile continued having to confine his vigorous barracking of the opposition to the division lobby. First he had some orders to give out at Somerleyton, where the Crossleys and indeed the whole village had cause to celebrate. Everyone was a-buzz with anticipation as they watched the delivery vans come and go and saw a series of marquees erected for the 21st birthday party of the young master, Frank Crossley. Villagers would still be telling their grandchildren about the parties, up to eighty years later. A report in the Gentlewoman newspaper described the events that started on Saturday 6th August with a 'huge' dinner party for family friends and relatives. 'Tents and marquees galore were erected for the week in the grounds, the whole of Monday, Tuesday and Wednesday being divided equally between the private house entertaining and the dinners and great ball for the tenants, as well as the huge children's fete in the park.'

Frank at 21 with his parents

Less fuss had been made of his sister's coming of age. Phyllis 'Noons' Crossley had become a debutante two years earlier at the age of 18. Monica talked about this finale to her sister's youth and education. 'For us it was pretty usual to remain with the governess - perhaps with a few outside classes included - until the age of 16 or 17, when we would be sent abroad, either with or without our governess, to be 'finished'- a ridiculous phrase! Our Miss Roberts took Noons first to Brussels and later to Weiman. After she came back from abroad she 'came out' which meant she was presented at Court, wearing the regulation long evening dress with a train and white Prince of Wales' feathers upright at the back of the head, and long white kid gloves, of course. She had to follow our Mother up a long gallery and into the Throne Room, where the King and Queen sat. A footman there took the train which had been carried over her arm until then, and Mum's name was read out, while she made her two deep curtseys to the Royal Couple, and then came the great moment, when the Official announced, "to be presented, Miss Phyllis Crossley", and my sister stepped out and made her two curtseys. Then they found seats in the Throne Room and sat to watch all the other people.'

After her presentation, Noons was propelled into Society. Monica recalled, 'She began a long series of balls and parties which were called 'the Season' which lasted well into July when the King left London, and gentlemen reverted to bowler hats instead of toppers, and we packed up to go home to Somerleyton until next February.' The daughter of Noons, Ursula Lloyd-Owen, adds that her mother was a shy girl and would not really have been comfortable with being put on show in this way. 'Mummy would have hated being presented at court, and being brought up with such a beautiful mother must have been daunting. I think Mummy was probably quite popular but not so beautiful that everybody was lining the streets to have a look at Miss Crossley. She was very intelligent and loyal, and she had a great sense of humour which must have come from Granny I think, because it could be quite caustic.'

It was not in the bright party lights of London that Noons found her future husband, Captain Evelyn Barclay, a member of the famous banking family. Ursula explains, 'Mummy was a great friend of his sisters and so spent a lot of time at Colney near Norwich, their family home. It was a fascinating place, they had a miniature zoo in the park there. Sadly the Barclays were great teasers of animals, and the eldest brother was teasing one of the lions with a bone one day and it went for him. He died as a result and so my father became the eldest. He and Mummy married during the first war and eventually they lived at Colney.'

The Crossleys' governess, having set Noons on the path to womanhood, was then responsible for Monica's early training, too. Monica said 'It has always been a marvel to me how Miss Roberts managed to teach us both, as my sister was not just seven years older than me, but also more intelligent. But she put up with me for 11 years and was particularly good at music and languages. The only thing she could not teach was painting.'

Part of Monica's apprenticeship involved mingling with the visitors when a party or fete was held at the hall for a charity or for the enjoyment of the villagers. She recalled, 'Very special events which took place on alternate years at home were the Workhouse Outing and the Flower Show. The former always brought a slight melancholy. Doubtless this would have been deeper, had I known more'.

'In those days it was very difficult for the working man to save anything out of his tiny wage, and if there were no children to help and no pension from the landlord, there was literally nothing when old age arrived, except the dreaded workhouse. One of the worst features was that married couples were separated there. Also they were issued with a kind of uniform - grey suits and black peaked caps for the men, and grey shawls and black bonnets for the women. They arrived sitting on Windsor chairs in farm carts. A few had wheeled chairs, to get them round the garden. There was always a Punch and Judy show, and of course a big tea which was served in a marquee in the deer park. And when they went away, every woman was given a packet of tea and every man a packet of tobacco. I don't remember anyone from our village going to the workhouse - I suppose they all had help from the estate.'

The flower show was a more light-hearted affair, said Monica, in spite of fierce rivalry between the entrants. People could become quite merry there. On one occasion Sir Savile was claimed for a dance by one of the older village women, and, much to the surprise and delight of the crowd, he accepted. Another great event for the villagers was the agricultural show, with competitions for the best poultry, sheep, pigs and cows, as well as horse jumping and displays of the heavy workhorses. Monica concluded, 'The last one I attended was on the eve of the Great War. The end of an era.'

By the summer of 1914, the country was being stirred by rumours of war, but, said one villager, few people thought it would really come. Nevertheless, in a frenetic whirl of activity, society hosts were holding lavish parties in all the large houses, as if the end of the world was in sight. Others were preparing for war in a more prosaic way. Young Frank Crossley had earlier joined the Ninth Queen's Royal Lancers and another local man, John 'Jack' Enticknap was his personal soldier groom.

The declaration of war came to the village like death itself; half-expected, certainly dreaded, and with no idea what lie beyond. Patriotic young men signed up for duty, hoping to come back soon and get on with the job of sowing seeds or digging the clay for new bricks, or preparing for the next season of calves and lambs. Keeping their emotions locked inside, they said goodbye to their families and took their first ever break from the country of their birth. The next four years would be no holiday.

Lady Crossley swung into action on behalf of the Red Cross. Her daughter Monica noted, 'Within a few days of the outbreak of war, my mother opened a hospital in Great Yarmouth, in a building formerly used for storing fishing nets. My sister made a very efficient quartermaster and of course I wanted to work there too, but was considered too young at 17 to be of any use.'

The Lowestoft Weekly Press dated 14 October 1914 carried a report on the first occupants of the 'Crossley Hospital', situated in the premises of Messrs Bloomfields Ltd at South Denes. It stated that one of the men had 37 wounds in his back and legs, and, more horrifyingly from Lady Crossley's point of view, he had come from her son's regiment. If she felt a sense of foreboding, she had good reason to do so.

Lieutenant F.S. Crossley and his colleagues in the Ninth Lancers had been sent to France in August 1914, and from there they moved onto the dreaded Ypres salient, a finger of allied-held Belgian soil surrounded by enemy territory. The action they saw there is detailed in a book about the regiment by Major E.W. Shepherd OBE, MC, in which he describes how the troops spent more of their time in trenches than on horseback. He quotes from the diary of one Francis Grenfell, 'Our men look funny sights trudging along with spades and things on their backs, and when they are mounted they are funnier still; if you see a man carrying a lance, sword, rifle, spade and pick he looks just like a hedgehog. But it is a jolly hard life for them to have to fight their way up to the line, then hold it, all the time cleaning and trying to look after their horses.'

At the Belgian village of Messines the men of the Ninth settled in, with few provisions and none to be found 'save indifferent champagne and some wine which seemed to have solidified in the bottles for some reason'. They dug more trenches, and off-duty officers found time for some pheasant shooting, but then they were on the move again and on the night of 30 October they were kept awake by the sounds of the enemy nearby on the Front. The next morning, the Germans attacked from all sides. When the Ninth rallied back near Messines three quarters of the officers and over a third of the ranks had become casualties. Lieutenant F.S. Crossley and others had been wounded and taken prisoner.

Frank's father, Sir Savile, was in France at the time, serving as a Commander with the Red Cross based at Boulogne. He had been refused a fighting commission on the grounds of his age and was hurt to have been sidelined at 57. A riding accident some years before had left him slightly lame but he was eager to see some action. The Lowestoft Weekly Press reported that he tried to reach his son, 'but was unable to get to him, owing to the fact that the village is held by the enemy.' It would be four years before they saw each other again.

Frank was taken with other wounded prisoners on an agonising journey in a cattle truck to hospital. His injuries were treated, but not with kindness. A surgeon removed the bullet from his leg without anaesthetic, and then put it back for a junior surgeon to extract again. Nevertheless Frank recovered and was wise enough to know that his only chance of survival until release was to get on with his captors. His natural charm helped him achieve this aim. Fellow prisoner Lieutenant (later Major General) C.W. Norman wrote in The Times, 'He had an amazing insight into and sympathy with the outlook of others, particularly of soldiers, by whom he was universally loved and later of all who served him. Even the German guards fell for him; an orderly in the hospital used to smuggle a bottle of beer into Frank's bed almost nightly on returning from his carousals in the town.'

No matter how much the Germans took a liking to Frank he suffered great hardships while imprisoned, not least of all hunger. When he had recovered his strength, he opted to work on a farm, where, he told a friend, he and his colleagues had been so desperate for food that they had begged for and been granted the body of a still-born foal to take away and eat. The confidante added that such experiences must have helped to compound his compassionate character, stating, 'You may be a Lord, but if you have had to put up with that sort of thing, I think it makes you less arrogant, and more appreciative about life.'

Frank's parents were naturally worried about him but they channelled their energy into good works. In August Sir Savile had gone out to Belgium and France with Sir Alfred Keogh, the surgeon-general who headed a Red Cross Commission to organise hospitals, transport for wounded, provisions and staff in tandem with the Order of St John and the Royal Army Medical Corps. They checked out rest stations and store depots, and they tackled the pressing need for ships and vehicles to ferry the wounded to places of safety. Using every ounce of improvisation they even set up two Hospital Trains equipped with stores from the now empty Paris Hotels and fully staffed with Red Cross doctors and nurses.

No one, not even the King escaped their determined efforts to ensure that fighting men were cared for properly. In November Sir Savile sent off an angry letter to the private secretary of King George V, protesting that 150 wounded Indian troops were being shifted from tents to a hospital ship before his Majesty's planned visit to Boulogne. The idea was so that the King would not see so many men in makeshift conditions under canvas. Lord Stamfordham wrote back to say the King had regretted to hear that men had been moved for his visit and that the issue had been brought to the attention of the military authorities, although the King 'was sure that this was done with good though mistaken intentions'.

Life in France was frustrating but not too uncomfortable for Sir Savile.

An acquaintance, Lancelot 'Lags' Gibbs, was serving in the Coldstream Guards and noted in his diary for 28 August 1914, '...no breakfast and no chance of food as far as we could see except for four dog biscuits I had collected. ...We came to quite a good camp on the hill about three miles from Rouen. We pushed off at once to the town for a bath and dinner. Sir Savile Crossley lent A.H. and self his room and we had a jolly good bath and shave. After a jolly good dinner and some Chateau Latour '98 we managed to persuade two frightful looking bounders in some 'Khaki Gamage' uniform with a Rolls Royce to drive us up, thinking we were on the Staff...Bed very sleepy and just a little drunk at 11.30pm!'

Sir Savile resigned his post as joint commissioner in December and returned home, where Phyllis had been hard at work. Their daughter Monica recorded, 'The Germans had dropped their first bomb from a zeppelin, very close to my mother's little hospital in Great Yarmouth. So the next morning she brought them over to Somerleyton, where we'd prepared the library to accommodate them. Then she opened a hospital at my aunt's big empty house, Cheveley Park, near Newmarket, where I was taken on as a 'tweeny' to do any unskilled work that no-one else fancied. This came to include beating mattresses, scrubbing lockers, carrying washing water, cutting sandwiches and cleaning and carbolizing the Theatre, before and after operations.'

Nurses and patients at Cheveley

A granddaughter has since suggested that Phyllis' role was probably much less 'hands-on', and more of a decorative nature. 'I can't see her taking away a bedpan or making a bed, she wouldn't have had an idea of how to make a bed. But she'd have walked through the wards and if they'd said "Oh isn't she beautiful", that would have been great.' Whatever her motives may have been, Lady Crossley received the CBE for her efforts.

Doctors and nurses with Phyllis, standing, front, at her hospital near Newmarket

Phyllis had commandeered the butler's pantry as an operating theatre and the estate's electrician had rapidly learned the art of X-rays. A shortage of doctors in the area forced the hospital to close in April 1917 but, said Monica, 'Maybe it was as well. For one reason, I think my Father, who had borne the brunt of the expenses except for a small allowance per man, would have gone broke.' Monica was probably right. The estate accounts confirm the heavy burden that Cheveley was putting on the Crossleys' finances. For every pound's worth of provisions allocated to Somerleyton, four times that quantity was going to Newmarket. In one set of accounts for 1917, provisions for the hall came to £27 while the cost of feeding the Cheveley inmates was put at over £300. It was a well-accepted fact that the government's allowance could never match the real cost of proper food and care for the patients, and income from the War Office for the same period was shown as £90.

Extract from Somerleyton accounts showing Cheveley expenses

Of course, Cheveley could not be blamed entirely for the sharp downturn in Sir Savile's finances. He had recently spent over £3,000 buying the Herringfleet Hall estate, which neatly fitted a gap in his Suffolk land holding. It was not a profitable time for farming but it made good long-term sense and the opportunity simply could not be missed. He had plenty of plans for making economies though and at Somerleyton Hall he had already signalled the end of profligacy by ordering the demolition of the stunning but so-costly Winter Gardens. The once glittering cavern became a heap of broken glass and scrap metal, while the statues were re-sited and the glorious fountain was sent up to Halifax to be put in the People's Park. There would be no more parties spilling out into its tropical splendour - in fact there would be far fewer parties altogether.

Much to the disappointment of Phyllis, the great London mansion in Carlton House Terrace was given up to the army during the war and the Crossleys moved to a smaller town house in Deanery Street. It had no grand ballroom, and there would be no more grand balls. Compensation in some measure soon followed.

In 1916 Sir Savile Crossley became a baron and thereafter he and Phyllis were titled Lord and Lady Somerleyton. Even then it was not a good time for having extravagant parties when so much poverty and tragedy was in evidence all around and besides, it was a time when many people were being honoured for helping their country in crisis. But quite apart from all the other pleasures his new status would bring, Savile welcomed the chance to voice his political opinion once more, and from now on, the highest officials in the land would have to take note.

Lord and Lady Somerleyton soon enjoyed two more celebrations, the weddings of their daughters, Noons and Monica. The Somerleytons had been happy with their eldest daughter's choice of a Barclay for a husband, but Phyllis had misgivings about Monica's match. She was to become Mrs Smith - not an inspiring title in her mother's eyes, and she would willingly come to share her new husband's profound religious beliefs. Phyllis, while happy to read out prayers for the wounded in her hospital, could not quite empathise with the idea of having priorities above those of beautiful possessions and a life full of leisure and fun.

Nevertheless, Monica was devoted to Captain Arthur Smith. He had come in as a patient and a measure of his mettle had been his refusal to allow the surgeons to amputate his shattered leg. He would suffer from the decision for the rest of his life, but he always walked tall, his pain only apparent in the slight limp he could not hide. He would make his determined way up the aisle on sticks, and Monica's eyes would shine with pride. In the second war he would be knighted twice in recognition of his distinguished military career, and his dedication to his family and those who served under him were matched by his allegiance to God. When he was released from hospital in 1918 he was stationed as General Staff Officer at his in-laws' former London home, the grand house at Carlton House Terrace. Not only had he taken Phyllis' youngest daughter, but perhaps worse, he was now giving out orders in her beloved mansion.

Monica's wedding, 1918

Lord and Lady Somerleyton may have lost two daughters, but at last they had their eldest son back when he was released from captivity at the end of the war. Frank Crossley returned home, a gaunt, thoughtful figure with a Military Cross for gallantry and a promotion to Captain. He knew that his experiences could have been far worse - at least he had escaped with his life. Sixteen men of Somerleyton are listed in the church as having given their lives in the conflict. The familiarity of those surnames adds poignancy to the knowledge that their forebears had been in the village for generations and in some cases their descendants remain there. Among them are Balls, Allum, Betts, Cole, Butcher, Kemp, Richmond, Rumsby and Wilson.

Over the coming years the reluctant witnesses of the war would stand in church and gaze at the role of honour, remembering the faces and praying for their souls. Estate painter Charlie Balls, his wife Ellen and their eight daughters would forever mourn the loss of young Charles, their only boy. Sam Cole the butler at Somerleyton Hall would write about the tragedy of losing his youngest brother Sidney, 'the baby of the family'. It was 60 years later when he still recalled the pain his mother endured. One former villager, Sir John Evans, kept a photograph of the 1913 cricket team - five of the members had died by 1919. John 'Jack' Prettyman was just one who survived the unspeakable horrors and only wrote about a fraction of his experience many decades later. His son David said, 'The only time he ever talked about it was on the anniversary of the day he was wounded. It was like a birthday, probably more important than a birthday. At the end of the story he would say "thank you for listening". He just wanted to get it off his chest. I know he thought he was lucky to have survived.'

Charlie and Ellen Balls with five of their eight daughters. Their only son was killed.

As the people of the estate began to pick up the pieces of their lives, Savile's public career was improving further still. He was made a Lord in Waiting to King George V, which required him to resign as chairman of the Crossley family firm, but the personal pleasure it brought him far outweighed the financial loss. Even so, economies would be made at Somerleyton Hall.

In 1919 Lord Somerleyton brought in his agent Kerry Rix and together they cast a critical eye over the estate plans, looking to trim away the outlying parcels of land. They identified a total of over 1,000 acres and as soon as an advert was placed in the newspapers about the intention to sell, offers and enquiries flooded in. Flixton House, the former home of his mother Martha, was sold quickly by private agreement, although a prospective purchaser argued that it was not worth half the valuation as it was in need of considerable attention and had not been painted for over seven years. No doubt Savile pointed out that many of his estate workers had been otherwise occupied during at least four of those years, serving their country.

Other holdings were likewise sold before the main auction, which took place at the Royal Hotel, Lowestoft in October. The remaining surplus land, over 800 acres including a market garden, dairy farm and manor house, went under the hammer.

Blundeston, Flixton & Oulton

NEAR LOWESTOFT, SUFFOLK.

Particulars and Conditions of Sale

OF CERTAIN

OUTLYING PORTIONS *of the*

Somerleyton Estate

COMPRISING

FOUR COMPACT FARMS

Known as "HOLLY FARM"; "The WHITE HOUSE
FARM"; "FLIXTON OLD HALL FARM"; and the
"DAIRY FARM," situate in the Parishes of Blundeston,
Oulton and Flixton. Also Cottages, Marshes, Arable
Land, Market Garden, etc., situate in the above Parishes,
the whole containing

804 Acres,   0 Roods,   23 Perches

WHICH

MESSRS. NOTLEY

Have received instructions to Sell by Auction, at the
ROYAL HOTEL, LOWESTOFT

On Wednesday, 1st October, 1919

At Three o'clock in the Afternoon,

IN ONE OR EIGHTEEN LOTS.

KERRY RIX, ESQ.,
Lord Somerleyton's Agent,
Somerleyton;

Messrs. MORGAN & BUCKINGHAM,
Surveyors,
King Street, Norwich;

Messrs. CADGE & GILBERT,
Of Loddon, near Norwich, Vendor's Solicitors.

Money was now spent on Somerleyton Hall, making up for the years when maintenance had become a low priority. In 1920 Savile cut another financial tie by having the banqueting hall remodelled, lowering the ceiling to create more guest bedrooms above and making the reduced room into a library. Lady Somerleyton could still host a ball in what was formerly known as the White and Gold Drawing Room, but the catering would be on a smaller scale from now on.

The grand banqueting hall before alteration

By the early 1920s Captain Frank Crossley was doing some socialising of his own and in particular he was enjoying the company of a certain young lady. Bridget Douro Hoare's parents lived at Welwyn in Hertfordshire, although the family spent a good deal of time in Norfolk where they had a second house and where relatives owned large tracts of land. Bridget's father was a keen sportsman as well as being an affable man with a varied mix of friends, so when their paths inevitably crossed Frank was easily attracted to the warmth of the Douro Hoares, and pretty Bridget attracted his special attention.

Whilst the family had no title as such, there was blue blood in Bridget's veins courtesy of an indiscretion by King George IV a century earlier. The royal link was on her mother's side. Her father, Douro Hoare, came from Quaker stock with Irish ancestors who had been given land by Cromwell. That inheritance amounted to very little by the time it had been subdivided by generations but the family were comfortable enough and Douro worked as a banker in London, culminating in his being made a Director of the Bank of England.

Douro, named after a Spanish river where his grandfather had been wounded in the Peninsular War, had been brought up in the midst of an extensive, happy family. He had 50 cousins and his father had over 70 so their house was almost constantly full. They divided their time between London and Marden in Hertfordshire and were frequently in Cromer, Norfolk, for holidays.

His parents were true philanthropists and Douro himself was proud to be related to the ardent prison reformer, Elizabeth Fry, and also to Sir Thomas Fowell Buxton, who had been instrumental in the abolition of the slave trade. He had other relatives with strong characters: an aunt who had married Sir Edward Parry, one of the first Arctic explorers, an uncle who died taking part in a steeple chase when aged well over 70, and another who swam in the sea at Cromer before breakfast, even when quite elderly. Douro's grandfather, Samuel Hoare, was such a devout man of his word that when he was robbed by a highwayman and promised to give all his valuables in return for his life, Samuel Hoare apparently called the brigand back when he found that he had forgotten to hand over his watch as well.

From these forebears, Douro had inherited admirable traits, as recalled by his sister, Louise, 'Douro was a very good eldest brother, I had many happy days alone with him seeing sights in London or following him round at Marden. He was very keen about the London Hospital and was on the committee there for about 25 years. Douro had inherited from my father very affectionate ways; as fathers they thought their children perfect and as brothers admired their sisters. I have seen the same trait coming out in my nephews, so much care and consideration for their womenkind.'

Douro and his wife Ida settled in Welwyn with their seven children of whom Bridget, or Biddy, was the fifth, born 20 October 1899. Her childhood was a happy one, basking in the love of her parents and siblings, but there was sadness in 1908 when her eldest brother died at 16 of diabetes, then untreatable. For Bridget and her family, their closer acquaintance with the mild-mannered and charming Frank Crossley, heir to the Somerleyton estate, was very much a silver lining after the dark clouds of war and depression. Their engagement created a soaring rainbow of excitement and anticipation.

By now Frank was active in the Territorial Army and at the end of May 1924 he became Major Francis Savile Crossley. Five weeks later he was addressed as such when he stood at the altar of St Marks Church in North Audley Street, London, to take Bridget Margaret Hoare as his wife. Decades later, a villager of Somerleyton wrote down his memory of that day, and this humorous anecdote in local dialect gives an evocative description of the event, unmatched by any society report.

'The whool wuld seemed tew be at the Chuch; St Marks it wor called in North Audley Street. Oi'm sure o' that cos oi lorst moi way an' a Bobby put me on the roight track arter oi'd arsked him where the big weddin wor bein held. Ar, there wor Dukes an Duchesses an harf the doirectors o' the Bank o' England, as well as MP's from all over the plairce. Moi hart, they wor a wunnerful good lookin set o' chaps and the lairdies wor dressed up tew the noines wi' orstrich feathers wairvin in all direckshuns. If oi remember roightly the Broide were all silver an' whoite an' carried a bootiful bunch o' red rooses. But that wor them little dairs what really took moi fancy. Ten little broidesmairdes there wor and foive pairges, all a-wearin green slippers. Some fooks rackoned that wor unlucky, but that doont seem tew hev brought them much harm, and in any cairse har Lairdyship int the superstishous sort. The orange trees on each soide o' the Charnsel wor marvellous tew; they fair maird our mouths water, noo mistairk.

Well, arter we'd had a good oyeful, we managed tew git a seat somehow. The singin wor grand, and win that wor all oover Lordie led his Broide down the Chuch, tew run the gauntlet o' the Guard o' Honour of Gal Guides wot wor a-waitin for em at the door. Oi've still got a footigraph o' the whool thing; Lordie's wearin a button'hool an a rare smart top hat, and they booth look as happy as larks.

Tew cut a long story short, we all went to Belgravia Square for a rare owd bust-up, but what with Cassano's Band an' the buckets o' bubbly oi doont remimber roight a lot about that.'

The newlyweds went to live at Caistor in Norfolk, just a short distance from Cromer where the Hoare clan gathered every autumn. There they were joined by a baby daughter, Mary, born in 1926.

Frank made one just attempt to follow his father and grandfather into politics. He contested Halifax as a Unionist in June 1928 but failed to become MP. Still, he had plenty to keep him busy at home; his beloved wife Biddy gave birth to a son, Savile William Francis, born 17 September 1928. The Somerleyton line had its new heir.

The patriarch of the family, Savile, Lord Somerleyton, was increasingly aware of his own mortality. He put himself under increasing pressure, drove himself hard, and occasionally let off steam at those around him. While he

Savile William Francis Crossley, aged 5 weeks

tackled the problem of income against expenditure, even resigning as a Lord in Waiting to seek lucrative directorships without success, he also kept up his attacks in the political arena, and had to be warned to show restraint when he saw the political colour red. There was an unspoken warning too. He began to suffer severe headaches, and booked himself into hospital for a brain X-ray. Whatever advice he was given, it was unlikely he took it, because he certainly showed no signs of taking life easy.

At Somerleyton Hall he had taken on a new agent since the retirement of Kerry Rix, and Captain Walter Flatt had the huge task of setting the estate to rights after the deprivations of the war years. He and Lord Somerleyton did not always see eye to eye, but Captain Flatt did bring the business back up to scratch. To alleviate some of the family's worries, it was agreed that Frank and Bridget should move into Somerleyton Hall, bringing with them their young children and close staff. It was an arrangement with mixed blessings, or, as another relative put it, 'For Bridget, it must have been undiluted Hell.'

It could not have been easy for the ageing Lord and Lady Somerleyton to adjust to hearing children's chatter and running feet, or to see Frank and Bridget welcoming the crowds of laughing, happy friends and family who came to marvel at the beauty of Somerleyton Hall. Their granddaughter Mary comments, 'I was about three when we moved to Somerleyton. I knew there was a need to move because my grandfather wasn't well and my father had to go and help run the estate. My parents slept in what was called the North Wing and they had a drawing room downstairs called the Green Room, while we children had the nursery on the top floor'.

'I do remember the difficulties of sharing the house, but my parents did manage to have house parties and they were allowed to have their friends to stay. They used to have these great big shooting parties and as children we were allowed to go out beating with the head keeper and that was a pride and joy. Then there would be a sort of party of the younger family in the Green Room and my grandmother would sit in her own sitting room, in what was called the boudoir, and my grandfather sat in the library with his friends, smoking. My brother and I used to go down between five and six in the evening. I had to dress in a frilly dress with white socks and red shoes and my brother was in a smart party suit and we were taken down to have what was called children's hour, playing with the parents. Then when Nanny came to collect us from their drawing room we used to be taken to say goodnight to our grandparents in their respective rooms.'

Mary recalls that her grandmother frequently criticised the way the young Crossleys were being brought up, but Frank and Bridget carried on regardless, casting off the old Victorian attitudes and bringing a whole new warmth to the Somerleyton environment. In 1932 another baby boy was born, Richard Nicholas, and the family was complete. In the midst of the younger people's joy there remained tension. The children loved their grandfather and were warily fond of their grandmother but for the older generation there was a sense that an era was coming to an end.

Billy with his father Frank and grandfather, Lord Somerleyton

Phyllis, Lady Somerleyton with her grandchildren Billy and Mary, 1930

Savile Brinton Crossley, first Baron Somerleyton, died at the age of 77 in a London nursing home on 25 February 1935. He had been taken ill while on a cruise with Lady Somerleyton to South Africa, and was brought back to London as quickly as possible. His agent at Somerleyton, Captain Flatt, received a telephone call, and, he said, 'Her Ladyship rang through to say he was better and could I come up - but not to talk business. I knew I could not fulfil that as he would force my hand, so I did not go but I sent the butler up with his letters. In the February her Ladyship rang through to inform me of his death.'

Obituaries in The Times and in the local press describe the funeral, attended by hundreds. Behind the scenes, Captain Flatt had left nothing to chance. 'His Lordship had wished to be buried at Somerleyton and to be carried on a farm wagon. I immediately thought that as this was winter and we had had snow, I better rehearse and time the whole thing, which I did, and I am more than glad I did it because I found in the hall to have carried the coffin upstairs, the antlers on the walls and all sorts of things would have been in the way. So I decided to put the coffin in the passage leading to the billiard room. On the day of the funeral we had two wagons with horses, the first being with the coffin and the second with wreaths and we proceeded down to the church.'

Neither of Savile's sons could attend. Frank was abroad and Jack was

The funeral procession led by (left to right) Captain Evelyn Barclay,
Sir Arthur Smith, Captain Walter Flatt

seriously ill in a nursing home. It was left to the sons-in-law and Captain Flatt
to walk the last journey with him. Countless cars followed them and again
Captain Flatt had prepared for any eventuality, stationing horses in the woods
in case any vehicles became stuck in the snow. The cortege reached the graveside
and there the remains of the first Baron Somerleyton were eased gently down
into the grave, which was lined with moss, evergreens, arum lilies and daffodils.

As the earth entombed these harbingers of spring, his widow Phyllis
heard the drumming soil heralding her new status as Dowager Lady
Somerleyton. This was the autumn of her life; half a century had passed since
she had been likened to a soft, pure lily, and the years had not been kind.
Without great beauty or wealth she would now find it harder to attract attention,
but at least at Somerleyton, she could still demand it. She would return to the
hall to mourn, but she would not be moved.

Chapter 3

Lordie, Lordie

O n a gloomy day in March 1935 Frank Crossley, now Lord Somerleyton, stood beside the heap of wilting flowers that marked his father's final resting place and said a quiet prayer for the man who had left him everything. He had returned as quickly as he could from India but had missed the chance to say goodbye and he felt the burdens weighing heavily on him. This would be one of his few opportunities to grieve, for now he would have to take sole charge of business and at the same time lift the spirits of his staff, tenants and families of Somerleyton estate.

Frank was himself middle-aged now and care lines were already apparent in his tanned face. His lazily-sloping left eye tended to squint as if he was struggling with all the emotion inside him, and the figure hunched inside his overcoat was as thin as a shooting stick. Fate of birth meant that at this point in time he was master of all he surveyed - the woods behind him were all part of his estate, also the lush pasture and parkland alongside him, and even this wind-whipped churchyard now came under his responsibility. But somehow he could not entirely see it as a privilege. Along with great wealth and power, he had inherited the old mantle of noblesse oblige and there were hundreds of people already looking to him not only for their livelihood but also for comfort and guidance. In higher society, people would be watching to see if he lived up to his father's great success in service to politics and the King. Times had changed though, popularity did not guarantee wealth, and in all honesty, Frank didn't see the point of it all. His priorities lay closer to home.

First of all there was a matter of urgency to deal with, and he was thankful to be in time for this family duty. Jack, his amiable, incorrigible brother was seriously ill in a London sanatorium and had lain helpless while their father was being buried. The sparkle had gone from his mischievous blue eyes and any old difference held between the brothers was forgotten in the crisis of his terminal illness. Now Lord Somerleyton wanted to bring his frail, fading sibling home.

Jack, born the Honourable John de Bathe Crossley in 1893 had always been the more handsome of the two brothers and had arguably been the favourite of their mother Phyllis, who saw her own zest for life and wicked sense of fun reflected in his easy, mischievous smile. Throughout his life, as second in line to the Baron's title he had been given less attention but more freedom, and any frustration he might have felt at being second fiddle was exorcised in bursts of athletic energy. As a lad he had been adept at climbing the roof of the Somerleyton laundry, much to the fake annoyance of portly Emma Cory, the head laundry maid who adored the cheeky boy. He would scramble up the thatch and set traps to catch sparrows, which his younger sister Monica would pluck for a pie.

As Jack grew up it became obvious that his talents lay not in paper and ink but in track and field. At school he used his aerial skill on the sports field and at university in Oxford he gained his 'Blue' for the high jump. He was chosen to represent his country in the high jump at the 1912 Olympic Games, although he was kept in reserve and denied the chance to stand tall on the winner's podium.

Back home in Somerleyton he had indulged in his love of speed at the wheel of his car, persuading his mother to take up his challenge and forget her dignity for a moment's wild fun in the passenger seat. The gatekeeper's son, Bertie Butcher smilingly recalled, 'My mother used to have to be ready to open the gate whenever someone wanted to go in or out. The chauffeurs used to pip their horn, but we always used to know when Jack Crossley come away from the hall. He had an old fashioned motor, damn great brass lights on the front, that was chain-driven at the back axle, and that used to rattle and roar. You'd hear him start away from the hall and we used to run out and open the gate. You'd hear him bloody miles!'

At the outbreak of the first war Jack had joined the Suffolk Yeomanry and he was sent to the Front in 1915. He served in Salonika, Gallipoli, Egypt and Palestine, and the sociable young soldier gathered friends wherever he went. In 1918 and now bearing the title of Captain Crossley he left the Western

Front where he had watched in eager fascination as the swarms of British biplanes droned overhead. He joined the Air Force, itching to get his hands on a joystick and get up there among the clouds. He grudgingly accepted the need for proper training but offered to go anyway as a mechanic, desperate to climb aboard one of the great, lumbering Handley Page bombers that were pointed at Berlin. There was no need for his help though, the war ended and once again his chance to excel was thwarted.

Jack and his new bride at Somerleyton Hall

So keen was he to prove himself, he set his own seemingly impossible challenges. On one occasion during the war he had bet fellow officers that he and his horse between them could jump 12 feet high. Jack cleared 5'11 himself and, mounting his horse, jumped 6'2 to win the bet by a mere inch, and admiration in far greater measure. He savoured the rare, sweet moment of success.

Jack was a man who advocated love rather than war and his magnetic charm had given him every opportunity to woo and win a beautiful partner, even if he had no great title or estate to tempt them with. He chose to marry Dorothy Caley, a Yorkshire girl with wealthy connections, and the couple produced two sons, Tony and Charles.

Jack became active as president of the local British Legion branch and took a keen interest in politics, happily engaging his staunchly royalist father in heated debates. All went well for a time, with the family living as tenants of Somerleyton Estate at Caldecott Hall, a six bedroom farmhouse with over 800 acres of land, and Jack playing the part of gentleman farmer. It turned out to be a role he was simply not cut out for.

Money came and went, but on balance more went than came. Jack invested in the very latest farm machinery and the best quality stock, but his judgement was rarely based on sound business principles. His father Savile tried first to advise and later to direct, to no avail. In 1922 Jack moved his family to the newly refurbished Lake Cottage on the estate, and Caldecott slipped further into decline. By 1926 the game was over and Jack accepted that it was time to cut his losses. Every piece of equipment and every cow, horse and hen was auctioned and in disgust, Savile sold off the whole Caldecott estate cheaply.

In that same year the country was locked in the General Strike and Jack, like many other gentlemen and peers, tried to 'muck in' and help keep the wheels of industry turning. Family stories tell that Jack tried his hand as railway porter but in no time had caused chaos by mixing up the farmers' milk churns at the station and sending the wrong ones back. It would have seemed like a minor problem to him, but not so to the farmers concerned and 70 years later it is still remembered.

Jack was typically unbowed by it all. When he wrote to his father to say he had personally been down a well at Lake Cottage to clear out some rubbish left by contractors, he signed the note 'Best love, your loving son, Jack.' In his mother's eyes he could do no wrong and she would back him in any way she could. While Savile and Frank insisted on being serious about money and estate matters, here was someone after her own heart, someone she could laugh and tease with, talk honestly about her love of gambling and high living,

Jack and his father, Lord Somerleyton

without being constantly reined in by purse strings.

In Jack's own household, Dorothy was less impressed by her husband's warmth towards others and in 1930 she divorced him. He had fallen in love with another lady and he re-married the same year, but first he took time out to work as a cowboy in America. There, apart from suffering in the cold climate and feeling appalled by his colleagues' cruelty to their horses, he apparently sowed the seeds of his early demise.

His second marriage was to Sibille Drummond, nicknamed Boojam or Boo in childhood by her South African nanny. She had been born at Kimberley when her father was a guard at the diamond mines, but the family estate was in England near Southampton and it was here at Stone Farm that the newlyweds settled. Again Jack took up farming, mostly on an aesthetic level, with a collection of Red Poll cattle, rust-coloured Suffolk Punch horses, and Rhode

Island Red hens. Life was colourful and fun again, and his happiness with Sibille was complete when a daughter was born, named Belinda. The little girl was just three when her father's health and energy suddenly dipped into decline.

Young members of the Crossley family were told that Jack had contracted Tuberculosis by chewing on contaminated grass while in America. All that Belinda remembers is seeing her father's wasted form lying between the stark white sheets of a London Sanatorium. She gave him a white fluffy toy dog to keep him company. His heart must have wept.

He would never see his wide-eyed daughter grow up into a fine lady, the wife of Lord Montagu of Beaulieu, and with two beautiful children. He would have enjoyed the irony of seeing his first wife Dorothy become good friends with his second wife, Sibille. Such was their understanding that Sibille virtually adopted his sons while Dorothy took up solitary residence at the International Sports Club in London.

The only consolation he would have in the last weeks of his life was to be cared for by his devoted mother, with all the comforts money could buy. His brother would be busy, but he would find time to come and stand awkwardly by his bed, and perhaps without speaking they would understand each other, the one who had had all the attention and the inheritance, the one who had had all the freedom and fun.

When Jack lay quietly in the pristine sheets, drifting into his last days in Somerleyton Hall, he would have felt the presence of his late father and known that they would soon be reunited. Just one month later, in June, his body was laid to rest near to Savile.

Bereavement did nothing to unite Jack's loved ones. At the funeral, his family ignored his new wife and after the service it was the Somerleyton butler, Sam Cole, who took Sibille back to his pantry and gave her a fortifying double brandy.

There was no doubt about her late husband's popularity though. According to one message on the floral tributes, Jack Crossley was 'one of the best'. His love life had scandalised the neighbourhood and he had blotted the sacred family honour, but his death spread a chill where once there had been warmth and magic. A card of condolence which his daughter Belinda still keeps close to hand states; 'With deepest sympathy to a devoted master and dear friend from all at Stone Farm. We loved him dearly but God loved him more.'

The profound grief that touched everyone at Somerleyton Hall was veiled behind guarded expressions. The Crossley children, hardly aware of what death meant except in relation to hunting and shooting, could not have truly understood why their parents and grandmother seemed troubled and even more distant than usual. They missed their grandfather, of course, and they were sad that Uncle Jack had gone, but the rituals of grieving were not designed to allow for outbursts of emotion. Mary was nine at the time of Savile's passing and one memory is particularly vivid. 'I remember first of all we had been very sad when the king died and we had to wear mourning for three months. And then about the same time my grandfather died and so it happened all over again – mourning for three months. One day I was taken to London in a chauffeur-driven car and I was left in a flat with Granny and I can remember her being completely enveloped in black with widows' weeds. And of all horrible things, she had whitebait for lunch and I'd never seen a whitebait before and I couldn't eat it. So widows' weeds and whitebait have always gone together in my mind after that.' Mary shudders again at the gruesome vision.

Phyllis' appetite may not have been affected by her bereavement, but belts would have to be tightened at Somerleyton if they were to meet the swingeing blow of death duties. Savile's vast stores of wealth had dwindled by the time of his death and there simply was not enough spare cash to cover all the demands. Frank had to find things to sell.

Most of the Somerleyton treasures were held in trust and could not be touched - it was a normal safeguard against any heir being wasteful and losing everything. But Frank needed money not for gambling or the good life, he simply had to hand it over to the Treasury. In June 1936 Sotheby's sold various items at auction, raising £780 and in the following month another 24 lots went under the hammer at Pall Mall in London. The catalogue included cabinets, chairs, mirrors, a piano, items of French furniture and firescreens. Four of the lots had a probate valuation beside them but the price they realised fell far short each time. Just over £200 was realised. If they were to keep Somerleyton Hall and Estate going, there would have to be more economies.

At times it seemed to Frank that his inheritance was just a great white elephant with a voracious appetite, and to cap it all, he was not even keen on the status of Lord of the Manor. He was far happier when dressed in his oldest clothes for scruffing around in, and never more content than when he could be doing some manual jobs on the estate. He would gladly pick up a scythe and swing it with a vengeance at the nodding grass, or go laying hedges or pruning trees. Sometimes he would escape into the woods and seek out some of his men for 'a yarn'. One former employee commented, 'the trouble was, he used to stay over lunchtime, and he'd never brought any of his own. So the men used to offer him some of theirs and he'd happily share their bread or whatever, but he didn't realise how hard up they were, that was all they had.'

On more than one occasion a visitor to the hall asked directions from a man whom they took to be an estate worker and only discovered his true identity later, when they were told it was in fact Lord Somerleyton. Similarly, Frank would often go to farm sales with his butler and friend Sam Cole, and people would assume that the tall, distinguished manservant was the baron. When they stopped for lunch at a pub on the way home, Frank would keep quiet and just listen to the rolling Suffolk accent, afraid that if he was recognised as a 'toff' he would not be able to blend in.

Frank - in his element on the farm

In 1935 Frank did appear at the House of Lords to be welcomed to his new title, but otherwise he tried to steer clear of pomp and ceremony wherever possible. Another employee, Ted Wilson, added, 'He used to grumble if he'd got to dress up and go out to some sort of a do. He'd say to Bridget, 'Why don't you go on your own", but the invitation would be for two, so he'd have to go.' Frank loved his wife Bridget dearly and she in turn loved the glamour of being a Lady, so there had to be some compromises. They duly attended state occasions like the coronation of King George Vl and later Queen Elizabeth ll, but the obligatory crown and robes rested uneasily on Frank. The softness of velvet and fur suited Bridget much better, she wrapped herself in the scarlet cloak and stepped out with an instinctive grace. She was not classically beautiful, but her attractive face glowed with an inner warmth and her china-blue eyes could capture a man like quicksand.

Whether it was lunch at the Palace or tea at the Ritz, Bridget never looked out of place. But she was equally at home in the poorest estate cottage, where she took her children to visit the elderly and sick, and she was constantly on the look out for ways to help. She was finding her feet as Lady Somerleyton and the tenants soon recognised that her style was very different from that of the dowager. She simply loved people.

Lady Somerleyton, or Biddy to her friends, was determined to make her mark in the village. While others quailed under the eagle-eyed disapproval of the formidable rector's wife, Biddy would take her knitting into church and make the most of any lulls in the proceedings to add a few more rows. Nurserymaid Violette Beechener added that her ladyship was less keen to finish her garment than raise eyebrows; she loved attention and enjoyed the frisson of daring disobedience in the eyes of stuffy authoritarians. As Violette commented with a smile, 'anything to cause a sensation.' It was harmless fun, and no doubt only added to her popularity among the less rigid members of the congregation.

Bridget was especially fond of older people, and she kept an eye on every one of them as if they were a great family of grandparents. She took all the village spinsters under her wing, calling them her 'unclaimed treasures', and later on she would have tea parties for them. Bridget also had a lifelong desire to help young girls make the most of their opportunities and she vigorously promoted the Girl Guide movement as an excellent combination of teamwork, fresh air and exercise. Here she had Frank's complete support, and he soon followed her lead. It suited him to be involved in local Scout groups - he was expected to do charitable work, and in scouting he could play a major role almost from the comfort of his own home.

Bridget was keen to help anyone in need, and usually she knew someone who could be called upon for a favour. Her disarming, intense blue-eyed gaze rarely met with refusal. However her good nature meant that she was often in danger of being caught up in neighbourly disputes, and there were times when one resident would write to complain about the conduct of another, expecting her to intervene. Then there were some occasions when the recipient of her help might have said she was generous to a fault. 'She was determined to help,' explained one former resident. 'And because she was so close to the community she always heard about anyone in need. But sometimes people like to do their own thing, go about it in their own way, but she wouldn't hear of it. If she couldn't get the thing done for nothing by someone, she'd pay for it herself. But more often than not she knew someone who knew someone.'

Resentment would be too strong a word for the resistance some felt towards her well-intentioned advances, and in most cases gratitude would be the sentiment. There are too many cases to mention, but the list would include the woman who was given a holiday for the first time in her life, the young man steered out of trouble by being given a secure job in the gardens, or the child who needed surgery to correct a curvature of the spine, but couldn't be given a date in the foreseeable future. Once Lady Somerleyton intervened, he went into hospital within a few days.

Bridget's kindness and generosity overflowed whenever she heard of a needy case. It was her driving force, the reason for getting up in the morning, and she would have been horrified to think that her fixing was ever misplaced. But sometimes, on rare occasions, it could be, like when she arranged adoptions between girls who were 'in trouble' and childless couples. She only ever saw the polite, friendly face of her acquaintances and, seeing people with a rose-tinted glow she might not always have been the best judge of character. Without a real understanding of the complexities of people's deeper nature, it seemed a simple matter for her to take a baby from one woman and give it to another. If the arrangement didn't work out, there was no Social Services agency to step in. In most situations, if Bridget couldn't help, nobody could.

Bridget saw good in everyone, and that naivety could sometimes be amusing as well as charming. She was an erratic driver, even though she was awarded a certificate for advanced skills at the wheel. The problem was, she had too much else to think about all at once. Those who were offered a lift were caught on the horns of a great dilemma over whether or not to accept. One passenger recalled, 'We were driving through a village one day and the road went through a narrow part with high banks either side. We came up to a school crossing and the lollipop man stepped out, but she simply didn't see him. In panic he scrambled out of the way and gesticulated, but she waved and smiled, commenting on how friendly the locals were!'

With such a vivacious, busy mother and hardworking father, the Crossley children, Mary, Bill and Nicky had to find their own amusement. They were not short of company with a nanny, nurserymaid and governess to attend to their needs, and they enjoyed watching the staff at work. Nancy James, a former gardener, recalls that whenever she made a bonfire of leaves and rubbish the children would come rushing out at the first whiff of smoke. In the hall they would chat to the footmen and play games with the butler, as long as their starchy governess wasn't around to disapprove. When Sam Cole was butler, he worried about their apparent lack of affection and had to curb the urge to give them a hug. He loved them almost as much as his own children, but he could see that they were being brought up to be independent and emotionally restrained. Their future success in the upper echelons of society would depend on it.

Nicky, aged two

That didn't mean they had any special favours. In church, the rector's harsh wife, whom the village children nicknamed 'the Hawk', would stalk around the pews ready to tap any little Sunday School child who turned its head. A witness adds 'she even did it to Lord Somerleyton when he was a little boy, and even though he was there with his nanny or governess, she would tap him. She was a shocker!' Contemporaries of the Somerleyton children all agree that, although there was a world of difference between the rich and poor families, nobody envied the little Crossleys; their smart clothes were no compensation for their restricted lives. Sam Cole's daughter Rowena adds,

'When I heard that Billy had 6d a week pocket money, I said to my father, "it's not really fair that I should have the same amount as he does, I'm much older than he is and my expenses are far more." So my father said, "I think maybe you've got a point there" and gave me another 3d.'

Bill could not mix with the village children and his relationship with his siblings would soon change as they too went their separate ways. In keeping with tradition, Mary was to continue being taught at home until she was ready to be 'finished' abroad. In those days there seemed little point in giving girls any great academic skills. In writing about life for masters and servants, author Jessica Gerard said in her book entitled Country House Life, 'Many upper class parents believed girls needed to learn only enough to attract a husband, by being a pleasing companion, reasonably well-informed and able to entertain with charming accomplishments.' Mary would certainly gain all these features, but in time she would decide for herself that she wanted more from life.

For Bill and his brother Nicky there was to be a different path, which took them off at a sharp tangent from the one they had been happily trundling along. Jessica Gerard suggests that the nursery regime with doting nannies led the boys to receive a nasty shock when they moved on to private school, as education for small boys then meant a rapid toughening up process. Lord and Lady Somerleyton, had arranged for their sons' progress accordingly. As Gerard put it, 'Only the boarding school regimen, parents believed, could harden a boy and inculcate the public-school ethos of independence, stoicism, courage, honour, loyalty and manliness.' So in 1937 Bill Crossley, heir apparent to the Somerleyton barony, was sent off to Reigate in Surrey, to St David's school at the age of eight.

It has been suggested that the governess' strict and inflexible style of teaching had been counter-productive, leaving Bill reticent in class, but he has no recollection of reported scenes of distress when the new term came around. His memories are happy and humorous. 'I remember St David's', he says, 'because we wore such funny clothes. We wore bowler hats and plus-four suits.'

Sadly, the head teacher signed up for the Irish Guards in 1939 and was killed at the start of the Second World War. His school closed and the children were scattered elsewhere. Leaving his friends, Bill moved to Ludgrove in Wokingham, Berkshire.

The outbreak of war had come as no great surprise to anyone, it had been predicted for months and some saw its potential long before that. For those who had served in the first conflict with Germany, there was a sense of disbelief that it could happen again so soon and all the visions of horror and deprivation came back to haunt them. Lord Somerleyton was too old to be called up and his sons too young, so there was less chance of family tragedy at Somerleyton Hall, but there was more than enough to do for others less fortunate.

The family soon made way for troops and war wounded soldiers, squeezing themselves into a quarter of the hall. In the early days there had been evacuees from Dagenham in Essex. The Somerleyton children had mixed feelings about those newcomers. They were delighted at the prospect of so much company, but they had never been in such close contact with the kind of poverty that city children knew. Apart from the fears of lice and germs, they were amazed by their living arrangements. Bill recalls, 'all the houses round here were allotted evacuees. We filled the whole of one wing with them and when they came they all had labels on. Each person was given a mattress each, but we soon found some of the families sleeping together on one mattress, they weren't used to having a bed each.'

The families themselves found their new surroundings lacked what they considered to be the comforts of home. One villager commented, 'It was a disaster. The first thing they looked for was a fish and chip shop, which of course we didn't have. They just didn't know what to do with themselves out here in the country.' That first wave of refuge seekers were soon relocated when there was talk of an invasion along the east coast, making Somerleyton a possible target.

Bill was only home for the holidays, before returning to Berkshire. His school was a long way from Somerleyton and the wartime meant that his busy parents only made the trip to visit him once a term. But he insists 'I was very happy there.' Shortages and rationing were rife even at the most affluent schools, and Bill adds, 'One of the funny things I remember is we all had to bring our own jam back, you know, because nobody had much to eat. My mother sent me back with fig jam, which nobody liked at all and of course I took enormous offence because no one ate it. I brought pounds and pounds of it back. The boys were probably quite right, it was rather like syrup of figs.'

Bill is philosophical about the harsh school regime, which included beatings by the headmaster and bullying. Then it was simply considered to be the norm, and indeed it was just the same at Somerleyton School, where the punishment book still exists to tell the tale. At his next school, Eton, he was all too aware of the inconvenience of war as the students were constantly bundled into shelters whenever the area around them including Windsor Castle was targeted. He said, 'Obviously everybody got exhausted getting down to the shelter and coming up again and down again so eventually the parents agreed that the children needn't go down to the shelter except when there was a serious raid on.'

Towards the end of his school career, Bill took on the job of ARP messenger; with a blue uniform and a gas mask, he had to sleep in the school office once a week in case of an emergency. He smiles, 'I don't know what I would have done if there had been a crisis, but I don't think I ever had to deal with one.'

Meanwhile, Lord and Lady Somerleyton rarely had time to sit down at all. 'My mother was marvellous, she was very well respected,' Bill says of Bridget. 'She was 24 hours a day on WRVS and Red Cross and everything else, and my father too, he was very busy in the Home Guard and other wartime occupations. When I came home they were all very busy, they didn't have a lot of time for us and quite rightly so.'

Frank, Lord Somerleyton and son Bill   *A moment of light relief*

In the midst of all the upheaval and the moving into smaller quarters, the dowager Lady Somerleyton, Phyllis, had decamped to Sidmouth in Devon. Up until then her icy presence in the hall had caused untold strain on the family, although she did spend every winter abroad and took many other trips to stay with friends and family. But in her last years she had less and less family to visit, and she was becoming increasingly fretful. In 1941 she was very concerned about her son's health as Frank had been ill with a bout of pneumonia. She wrote to the agent Walter Flatt, 'I have been terribly worried about his Lordship, knowing more about lungs than most people, having only one myself... Five doctors had given me up...my temperature was 103 and I was pretty nearly dead, after a major operation and then double septic pneumonia and pleurisy.' Phyllis was in fact referring to her loss of a kidney due to peritonitis some 30 years earlier. The passing years had caused her to confuse her organs. She continued in her letter, 'If they insist on coming (to visit) by train *do* see that his Lordship is thoroughly wrapped up, he ought to wear a really *warm* woollen under vest, or a pneumonia jacket under his clothes'. As well as this motherly advice, Phyllis went on to give Captain Flatt her opinion on the state of the war in general and the Irish Prime Minister in particular. 'I wish they would bomb Dublin flat, but they won't, as I feel sure Germany has an understanding with that traitor de Valera, and will use the Irish ports as a jumping off place for England.'

In another letter Phyllis described how she was kept awake at night with enemy aircraft flying over, heading for targets in Wales, Merseyside or Bristol. 'It's wearing to the nerves,' she wrote, 'when one is all alone as I am, and I get panicky about his Lordship.' But Frank was too busy to keep writing to his mother and she again pressed Captain Flatt for news of home. In February 1943 she complained, 'I wrote to his Lordship 10 days ago, but have had no answer, I have had no letter from anyone at the Hall. Today is the 8th anniversary of his Lordship's death, I am thankful he did not live to see this war'. She wrote of the German 'fiends' bombing London and added, 'Had they got into the West End, we might all have been wiped out, as the two boys, Lord and Lady S., Lord and Lady Grimthorpe, two of their children, Sir Arthur and three of his were all lunching side by side at the Ritz.'

The Somerleytons were trying to maintain some vestige of normality amidst the mayhem, but their circumstances at the hall were much reduced. They hardly had room to spread out and there were hardly any servants left to take care of their needs. Fit young girls were being better employed in nursing or in keeping the factories and farms operating, and the able-bodied young men had mostly been called up. While Lord and Lady Somerleyton's part of the house could no longer be kept so scrupulously clean, in other areas it had to be perfectly sterile. There the reek of disinfectant had replaced the delicate perfume of polish and the fine furnishings had been put into storage as broken men were carried in to the state rooms. Frank and Bridget's daughter Mary said, 'First of all the house was a sailors' convalescent home for a few months and then it was an advanced dressing station, and occupied by the Royal Army Medical Corps. It was full of troops all through the war – about 120 soldiers. They were living in the stable flats and in the stable yard and they had nissen huts as well. The big rooms in the house were like hospital wards, really. It made life very restricting for us and of course my mother was out the whole time doing WRVS work or Red Cross or working in the canteens like at the Sparrow's Nest in Lowestoft. Everybody mucked in, there was no question - all her friends, everyone. As soon as I was 17 I did – I ran the local guides for a bit and I went on a first aid course and then went in as a Naval VAD.'*

With soldiers all around the area, it was inevitable that some of them would form attachments to local girls, and some later married. Lord Somerleyton became alarmed at his innocent daughter's liaison with the young men and she was soon summoned for a 'talking to'. Commenting that her overriding memory of childhood is of her extreme loneliness Mary continues, 'I was just 13 when the troops came and it was so exciting to have all these young people about, they can't have been more than 18 or 19. That first winter of the war we had a lot of snow and they used to have snowball fights with my brothers and me. Then one awful day 'Coley' the butler came and said to me, "Miss Mary, his lordship wants to see you in the study." So along I went, and it was quite fierce being sent for to the study, but that day my father gave me my first sex education lesson, as it were. He said, "Mary, I hear you've been playing with the soldiers". So I said yes, and the boys had been playing with them too. But he said, "Well, you're not to play with the soldiers any more" and when I asked why the boys could but not me he answered, "Because you're a girl, and because I say so. Now go away."

Mary tried to carry on her friendships when her parents were out of the way, but someone obviously informed on her and she was packed off to boarding school. She concludes, 'I have to say, I never remember hearing anyone swear or anyone trying to take advantage of me. They all behaved impeccably.'

Her father Frank did recognise that the young soldiers were homesick and when the air raids started around Somerleyton, he saw their fear, too. One former servant said, 'He used to go out and talk to the guards while the planes were coming over. He was warned not to, but he said, "those poor boys are probably frightened out of their wits. It's still my house, so I'll do as I please." All the commanding officers could do was ask him to wear a tin hat.'

Life had become especially tough for the few remaining servants at Somerleyton. Butler Sam Cole wrote in his memoirs, 'The hall was taken over

*VAD - member of Voluntary Aid Detachment

as a military hospital. The footmen both left to join the forces and many of the other staff left to do war work. It soon became plain that my job as a butler was coming to an end. The family retained part of the hall and still did quite a bit of entertaining and I struggled to keep things going single-handed. It was very difficult and I became very tired and depressed. I gave up the job and moved to Norwich…it was a wrench to leave my mother and the village which had been our home for so many years.'

Sam's dignified presence was sorely missed, although his close friendship with Frank had at times been a source of niggling jealousy for Bridget. She had no taste for boating and setting pike traps on Fritton Lake, but when the boyhood pals set off on such missions, she had resented being left out. Her underlying feeling had surfaced when Sam had argued against some of the heavy, dirty tasks now expected of him and she had no sympathy at all for his weak heart, which had been damaged by illness in the first war. Buckling under the strain of working up to 15 hours a day and knowing that his wife often cycled out to the hall in freezing conditions to ensure he hadn't collapsed somewhere, Sam finally bid her ladyship goodbye.

It is unlikely that Frank knew about the last heated exchange between Sam and Bridget and he was lost without his butler's steadfast support, but his lordship held a deep affection for Sam to the end. Sam's daughter Rowena said, 'Our house in Norwich was bombed out and we had to go back to Somerleyton to live with my grandmother for a while. Lord Somerleyton saw me and said "I hear you've had a bad time." I told him we'd had the windows blown out and the door blown off and there was a big hole in the roof. Fortunately we'd been under the stairs so we were unhurt. To my surprise, I saw tears coming down his cheeks. "I'm so terribly sorry", he said.'

Around the estate the agent, Captain Walter Flatt, was doing his best to accommodate the squads of troops who were camping out all over his territory. He felt at ease with military types and was glad to be of service whenever possible. But he dug in his heels when an RAF representative came looking for extra gun sites and aerodromes. Captain Flatt explained in his memoirs, 'One of their runways would have been 2,000 yards long and gone straight through the Somerleyton Hall gardens. We then went further into the estate and the man seemed to think this was where he wanted to come.' Captain Flatt pointed out that, with the sea on one side and rivers on the other sides, the estate was effectively on an island with only four bridges on to it, so it was highly susceptible to sabotage and flooding. He went on, 'That night I rang through to Lord Somerleyton who was in Scotland and told him he better get quick on it and bring what influence he could to bear on it. The result was I never heard a further word about it and they eventually went to Ludham, the other side of Yarmouth.'

It was not that either Captain Flatt or Lord Somerleyton was reluctant to help the war effort, and both were key figures in the local Home Guard. Frank raised the company in 1940. Former member Clifford Dann likens his experience to that depicted in the television series 'Dad's Army'. He smiles as he recalls 'we had a stick each, that's all we had. We had to meet three nights a week at Ashby Church gate and we'd stand there and watch for the planes to come over. But we'd got no way of contacting anyone, only thing we'd got to do was run to the telephone box which was half a mile away. We never phoned anybody.' He continues, 'There was no uniform for us. But we'd meet right on time.' His wife Hilda interrupts, suggesting 'that was more for a yarn than anything else!' Clifford agrees. 'Yes, we'd be wondering where the next pheasant was going to perch for the night, that sort of thing.' Perhaps on reflection Lord Somerleyton was wise not to equip the men with guns.

Farmer's son David Prettyman has his own vivid memories of that period, when, he says, there was fierce rivalry between the home guard and the local air raid wardens. The latter were no better equipped for their job. He recalls, 'my father was an air raid warden and used to assist the policeman by riding around on a bicycle, blowing a whistle if there was any possibility of enemy attack.' Jack Prettyman would not be letting his time go to waste, though, says David. 'He'd have a bucket on the front with corn to feed the chickens which were living on the stubble field. He'd usually meet the policeman at some point on the journey and he'd ring his bell on the way back because the danger had passed.'

The stoical Suffolk spirit meant that life and work had to carry on regardless of irritating interruptions like air raids. David adds that his father, having survived two years in the trenches of the first world war, was unconcerned by anything he witnessed in the English countryside. He was angered though when there were stories of farm workers being shot at by enemy aircraft as they toiled alongside the threshing machine.

The occasional bomb drop caused no fatalities, but in 1943 the whole area became alert as impenetrable wire went up around Fritton Lake and there was talk of secret tests taking place. Ahead of the D-Day landings, the military wanted to try out amphibious tanks and they chose Fritton because it was relatively easy to seal off from prying eyes. The land included an area that was being farmed by David Prettyman's grandfather. 'He used to have to go to the Army to get permission to plough his own fields,' says David. 'One day when the sun was shining and the corn was ripe, grandfather was in the mood to cut the corn, but he was refused permission. He put on his parts to such an extent that one soldier was heard saying to another, "if he doesn't behave himself, I'll chuck him in the lake!"'.

There are sombre tales of a sunken tank and bodies still lying in the watery depths, but all evidence of the testing was removed when the war ended. Secret hideouts, explosive stores and an underground wireless station all became redundant in peacetime and one armoured tank was simply buried where it stood. The strange, barrow-shaped mound became naturalised with weeds and bracken, until it was completely camouflaged. Later still the remains of a USAAF P47 Thunderbolt aircraft were recovered from the lake, it was one of a pair that had collided with fatal results in April 1945.

Lady Somerleyton was awarded an MBE in recognition of her war service, and Frank received letters of appreciation from the King. They both continued to find new channels for their good works, and Frank, as County Commissioner of the Lowestoft Boy Scouts Association, offered the use of land at Fritton Lake for a Scout campsite. It became recognised as 'one of the best sites of its kind anywhere', according to a history of the area by Robert M. Pye. Lord Somerleyton was happy to see the young lads swimming in his lake, bird watching in the woods, or practising their field craft skills. He wholeheartedly supported the Scout Association's stated aim to '...promote the development of young people in achieving their full physical, intellectual, social and spiritual potentials, as individuals, as responsible citizens and as members of their local, national and international communities'. Frank later commented, 'I am quite convinced that Scouting is one of the finest movements there ever was.'

He could easily spare the land for this worthy cause, and in 1946 he added 100 acres to his landholding with the purchase of nearby Fritton Hall estate, which also bordered the lake.

Gradually the surviving menfolk returned home and everyone tried to settle down to some form of normality once again. But even though Somerleyton was much the same as it had been six years earlier, the people had changed. For many, their expectations had altered and now they wanted a better life for themselves and their children. Rowena Cole had been lucky – her father had earned enough as butler at the hall to provide a good education for her, but she says, 'there had been a tremendous waste of talent; there were some very intelligent children at our school and they just didn't have a chance. If their parents were earning 30s. a week they couldn't keep their children at school until they were 16 or 18. The girls were expected to go into service and for the boys it was farm work or gardening. But then they were beginning to have factories in Lowestoft and people were wanted in shops, so a few local people managed to get jobs in the town.'

This was bad news for Lord Somerleyton, who would have to improve his employees' conditions if he wanted them to stay. Like the Boy Scouts, ordinary working class people wanted to achieve their full potential, or at least, they wanted their children to have the opportunities they themselves had missed. The days of unquestioning loyalty were over.

In a letter to his former colleagues William and Violette Beechener, Sam Cole wrote, 'I don't often go to the hall and I never regret leaving there, although in the old days we had some good times...The butler is a discharged soldier, suffering with varicose veins, I should not think being there would be a rest cure for him.' The butler did not stay long and soon after, Lady Bridget asked if William Beechener would consider the job. He decided against it.

It was not only the working class who were beginning to take their lives into their own hands. Mary Crossley's progression to womanhood had gone off at a tangent and she had missed her chance to be a debutante in the old tradition. It didn't worry her a bit. She said, 'Any plan my parents had for me was finished by the war. I do remember afterwards they were quite keen that there should be a dance or something, but it didn't happen. My father wanted me to train as a nurse but I wouldn't do that. I didn't want to be a nurse in an ordinary hospital, I wanted to get into the Navy. At the time they didn't want any Wrens and all they wanted was someone to work for the Red Cross, to empty bedpans and that sort of thing. I wanted desperately to go to Australia and I applied and the draft came through for Ceylon. In those days you had to be 21 to go abroad without your father's consent, and he said no way was I going off with a lot of randy sailors so I wasn't allowed to go out of this country. I worked in RN hospitals until I got a class B release which allowed me to go to university and read sociology.'

'I had always been faintly left wing as a teenager and the war had encouraged that. My parents were both rather shocked when I went to university, they didn't know many people whose daughters went.'

In 1946 Phyllis, the dowager Lady Crossley, also decided that it was time for a change. In a letter to his friends William and Violette Beechener, Sam Cole mentioned that he had seen Phyllis in Norwich. 'The Dowager Lady Somerleyton came in the shop to see me yesterday. She looks an old woman now, she tells me she has bought a house at Newmarket and is moving there shortly.' Phyllis did indeed finally move her possessions out of Somerleyton Hall and it seemed as if she had found her perfect niche, so near to the home of racing. But still she couldn't settle. There was just not enough going on there for her liking, and visitors were few and far between.

She moved again, this time to London and there at least for a brief period she had some company when relatives were in the city on business. Her granddaughter Ursula Lloyd-Owen said, 'Even in her old age Granny enjoyed the company of men and she simply could not help flirting. When she had her flat in London my husband used to go and call in on her. He was a good looking young man and I expect they had a nice little drink together - it broke her day.'

Phyllis' great beauty had long deserted her and now her health was to abandon her too. On 2 December 1948 Lady Somerleyton wrote to William Beechener and said, 'You may have seen in the paper that Phyllis Lady Somerleyton died last week, she was only 79, but lately had not been at all well. She moved to London in September and I think it was really too much for her.' The following day the Lowestoft Journal printed an obituary, headed 'The Passing of a Great Lady'. It described Phyllis as 'a great lady, gifted with wit and conversational brilliance, with the result that she had many friends in every walk of life.' The article listed her public speaking success and her war work. Rather improbably, it added that she was a keen gardener. More truthfully it continued, 'Lady Somerleyton was very proud of her children, grandchildren

Faces of Phyllis —
as she would wish to be remembered

and great-grandchildren, of whom there are eight, but of them, no less than her friends and acquaintances, she was a strong critic, and those who failed to live up to her exacting standards soon fell temporarily from grace.' Finally, and with great insight the report concluded, 'She will never be forgotten and it can be said with truth that Phyllis, Lady Somerleyton, served her generation.'

Phyllis' remains were cremated in London and a simple memorial service was then held at Somerleyton Church. The attendance list shone dimly, there was no star-studded cast, and the dazzling spirit of a former bright light of society was extinguished with but a brief ceremony. Her fabulous collection of jewellery and clothes were bequeathed to those she considered her friends, and not to her family.

At the time of Phyllis' death, several of her relatives were abroad, including her grandson Bill, who had been called up for National Service. He said 'I had got a commission to the Coldstream Guards and in March 1948 we

Hon. Richard 'Nick' Crossley, 9th Lancers

all went to Palestine. Then later on I went in the advance party to Tripoli in North Africa and I believe we didn't come back until about the end of 1950, apart from leave and going on courses.'

Bill admits that his choice of the Coldstream Guards was a disappointment for his father. 'I think my father would have preferred me to go into the 9th Lancers as he had, but there were just as many of my family in the Coldstream. As it turned out my brother went into the Ninth so we satisfied everybody in the end.'

If Frank was upset by his son's decision, he might well have been nonplussed when on one occasion Bill was called upon to dress as a woman. Bill explains, 'We had a battalion concert about a lady Russian spy and I was chosen to be the Russian spy. I remember having to drink about half a bottle of whisky before I actually got on to the stage.' The act was received with rapturous applause, but Bill was not bitten by the acting bug, he says with some relief.

At Somerleyton, Bridget was always keen to dress up and play a part, and under her direction a number of themed fairs took place to raise funds for local facilities like the village hall and the church. Photographs of the Viking fair show Frank looking quite uncomfortable in his robes and felt hat, but at the 'Cries of London' event their son Bill happily joined in the fun as a travelling knife-grinder.

Although in some ways they were a world apart, Frank and Bridget held a deep love and respect for each other and they celebrated their silver wedding anniversary in 1949. To mark the event they commissioned a new village sign, designed to acknowledge the area's Viking heritage. They received countless gifts from friends and family, including a pair of wrought iron gates from the farm tenants. That choice certainly reflected the more prosaic nature of the latest Lord and Lady Somerleyton – it is hard to imagine the dowager, Phyllis having appreciated such a gesture. But practicality could have been Frank's middle name, and when he was explaining why none of his children were invited to the silver wedding party, he shrugged, 'They weren't there for the wedding, why should they come to the anniversary?'

Later the same year their son Bill came home to celebrate his 21st birthday with a grand party for family and staff, and the following year saw another major event in which hundreds of friends, relations and employees would take part; his sister Mary's wedding. Having graduated from university and gained useful work experience, she was at last ready to conform to her parents' view of normality. Or rather, she had fallen in love.

A wedding report in The East Anglian Daily Times explains the circumstances of her betrothal to Captain William Birkbeck of Westacre, Norfolk. 'It was a romantic match, full of family coincidences. The young couple met last January at West Norfolk Hunt Ball, where Lord and Lady Somerleyton had had their first meeting, and, a few weeks later, they became engaged on the same date as that on which Lord and Lady Somerleyton had become betrothed. Family history, too, repeated itself as the 6ft. 4ins. Guardsman walked down the aisle with his petite bride, for as far back as 1745 a similarly tall William Birkbeck had married a little ancestress of the bride's mother.' The pair shared other complicated family ties, but all that mattered to the Honourable Mary Crossley on Friday 7 July 1950, was to seal her happiness at the altar of St Margaret's, Westminster, and to share her great joy with over 800 guests.

The newspaper report described the exquisite scene, 'A diamond tiara which the bridegroom's mother bequeathed to him with the wish that it should be worn by his bride on her wedding day was among the jewellery worn by the Hon Mary Crossley... Round her shoulders and on her train was some beautiful 16th century rose-point Michelin lace which has been worn by brides in her mother's family for five generations, while her pearl necklace has been similarly used for four generations.'

Wedding guests from Somerleyton; (left to right) Pauline Cole, Joyce Roll, Peggy Smith, Jennifer Hook

'The wedding, which was one of the most colourful that even the West End has seen in recent years, re-united two of East Anglia's best-known families both of which came from the North of England several generations ago. Both too, retain a great love not only of their estates but of the people on them, and over 160 farm workers from the two villages were taken to London by special coaches and train to attend both the wedding and the reception afterwards.'

Frank enjoyed the celebrations and was pleased his daughter had made a good match. He had not always understood her or even approved of her course of action, but he could see that she had turned into a resourceful, popular lady who was a credit to him. For the time being there was no sign of his son and heir settling down. After flying home for his sister's wedding Bill stayed in the army for another six years after which he planned to travel the world, finding work and gaining experience of life wherever it led him. At the end of it all he would have the job and the lifestyle of a lord to come home to. Little did he know at the time, his father would have gladly swapped places with him there and then.

Somerleyton Hall was eating through his Lordship's money and still it was showing signs of wear. If it had been at all practicable, Frank would have stripped away the fancy facade and reduced the house back to its pre-Peto simplicity. He aired his thoughts to his agent, Tom Flatt, and they mulled over the possibility of Lord and Lady Somerleyton moving into a smaller house on the estate. Deep down, Frank knew his wife wouldn't hear of it.

He was right. Apart from wanting to keep her son's inheritance secure, Lady Bridget adored Somerleyton Hall, in all its ornate splendour. She thoroughly enjoyed every inch of its sumptuous rooms and private nooks and crannies, and she loved the garden with its shady alcoves where she could tuck herself away without fear of intrusion. Her own thoughts often strayed towards improving the grandeur of the hall, as the former agent Tom Flatt recalls. 'She had one idea of moving the clock tower from the stables into the middle of the hall. Anyway a contractor came over with an architect and that was discussed but they knew the score, they could see they were wasting their time. The man probably knew Lord Somerleyton or if he didn't he'd weighed him up, but he politely went through all the motions, what it was going to cost and so on. Anyway that all died a death.'

Somerleyton Hall before Peto's alterations in 1840's

Lord Somerleyton was doing his best to please Bridget, but their interests were often poles apart. He was keen on charity work but preferred to stay in the shadows, while her ideal position was definitely centre stage. In 1956 as president of the Lowestoft Old People's Welfare Committee she set about acquiring a grant for a new club building and duly got hold of £1500 from the King George Vl Memorial Fund. The project cost £8,000 in total, and Lady Somerleyton was publicly congratulated for being instrumental in its success.

In contrast, there was a scheme of world significance taking place literally on their own doorstep which Frank would help nudge forward, but his action would receive hardly any recognition at all, which suited him fine. Retired boat builder Doug Rushmer tells the tale. 'I was working for Christopher Cockerell at Oulton Broad, building caravans and hiring out boats. Then we moved to the old wherry dyke at Somerleyton and gradually we developed the place. We were building cruisers for our hire firm, Ripplecraft, but Mr Cockerell, who had been a designer at Marconi's, also owned racing boats and he decided to have a go at boat designing.'

Working to Cockerell's revolutionary and precise drawings, Doug would produce one boat a year in fine mahogany with brass trimmings. But his boss was determined to improve on the basic boat design and hit on the idea of pushing a jet of air underneath to speed it along. Doug continues, 'He bought a high speed launch and modified it, with a huge gas blower connected into the transmission system so that air was piped down under the boat to lubricate the hull. Its top speed went up from 14 to 24 knots. So then he did the famous experiment with a cat food tin and a piece of hose connected to a vacuum cleaner blower'. The first hovercraft was born.

Doug was sworn to secrecy and even his wife knew nothing about their tinkering in the shed at Somerleyton, but when Christopher Cockerell tried to market his idea, the men from the ministry put it on the 'secrets' list and effectively froze its progress. Some pressure was needed behind the scenes, and Lord Somerleyton was the man to help. Doug says, 'He was very interested and he got his friend Lord Louis Mountbatten interested. Lord Louis was a great go-getter, he got things done, cut through the red tape and got things moving.' To Lord Somerleyton's great excitement a small flying model was demonstrated on the lawn in front of the hall. Some time later, Christopher Cockerell's work gained him a knighthood, but the government reaped the financial rewards.

Lord Somerleyton was aged 70 at the time of the experiments and he had been suffering from rapidly declining health. Since a heart attack in 1954 he had tried to take life easier, but the work of a lord and landowner meant he could never really relax. One morning in July 1959 he set off for a meeting in London with a friend, passing pleasantries with his estate workers on the way.

Later that day, Lady Somerleyton received the news that her husband had collapsed and died outside the Bank of England.

Bridget was alone in the great house on that day. Mary was married, and Nick had also settled down. Bill was away, and the only people at Somerleyton Hall were a handful of helpers who were almost as devastated as the heart broken widow. In fact the whole Somerleyton community was stunned by the tragedy. They could hardly believe their friendly squire, whom they affectionately referred to as 'Lordie', would not be coming home. Also, they wondered what the future held in store for them.

The local rector paid great tribute to the late lord and said that at least it was comforting to know that Frank had been happy on the morning of his death 'because you just can't think of him without his smile and the merry twinkle in his eye.' But Frank had been troubled for some time, and knowing that his time might be short, he had already transferred the estate into his son's name to try to avoid another crippling tax demand. His son Bill had agreed to go into partnership with him, to learn to take over control of the business. The scheme was due to start within the next few months, but Bill's plans for an apprenticeship had been dashed. As the new Lord Somerleyton he was thrown in at the deep end, with only his mother for guidance and Tom Flatt the agent to hold out a branch of experience to him. His loyal staff knew their own jobs of course, but with all the vigour of a new broom, their employer would insist that the estate, and its workers, would have to adapt to survive.

From then on the estate changed immeasurably. While Lord Somerleyton set about making the business more profitable, he took on outside contractors and needed fewer and fewer staff. The nature of farming was becoming more intensive, and small tenanted landholdings were out of date. As each elderly patriarch died or moved out, economies of scale moved in. At the same time Lord Somerleyton set about catching up on the renovations which had been lacking at the hall and similarly he needed to improve living conditions on the estate if he expected his tenants to pay a fair rent. Some people would have the comfort of a proper bathroom in their home for the first time in their lives.

The dowager Lady Somerleyton stayed at her beloved hall until her son married Belinda Maris Lloyd in 1963 and then, determined not to see history repeat itself, she moved out with great reluctance and sadness. In a comfortable house in the village she would remain in most people's eyes the kind-hearted and much loved Bridget, Lady Somerleyton. It was she they would turn to for advice and help, and she still embraced every possible charity and needy case. When out and about in the village she would be chivvying young people along to help pick up litter or inviting the elderly round for tea. But when her guests were gone she was lonely, and she often found reasons to call up help from the hall whenever she could find a small task for someone. One handyman recalls being hugged when he arrived, and another smiles as he remembers that her Ladyship made him a cup of tea – it was about the limit of her cooking skills.

Bridget, Lady Somerleyton died on Boxing Day, 1983. Most of the older people of the village still have a special memory of her, of how she helped those in difficulty, or brought about a scheme to improve the social life of the local people. Some people say that she was at the heart of the community spirit, and that it died with her.

In reality, times had already changed and the people of Somerleyton had changed too. With fewer jobs available on the estate and higher expectations of careers and lifestyle, the old families were gradually moving out and being replaced by new faces and names.

Happier times - Bridget, centre, with guests at her daughter's
wedding, 1950

Lord Somerleyton accepts that he played a part in that social change, acting on government guidance. He said, 'New legislation has almost dictated that you should take land in, take it back into the estate rather than rent it out. The more than you take in, in theory, the better it is. But of course that has a detrimental effect too in that you lose families which have been farming here for generations, probably longer than my family have been here.'

So Somerleyton Hall stands as a symbol of continuity, while the estate marks the shifting fortunes and policies of successive owners, employees and politicians. And even if the scores of uniformed servants have long departed, Lord Somerleyton and his heirs willingly continue to serve Somerleyton, shouldering the enormous responsibility as their born duty.

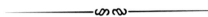

PART TWO

Servants' Tales

Chapter 4

The Upper Domestics

When Sir Francis and Lady Martha Crossley first moved into Somerleyton Hall they brought with them a small team of staff from Halifax, whose hearts must have sunk when they saw the enormous mansion. Standing alone and uninhabited, miles from the nearest town, it may well have represented more of a prison sentence than a promotion for the three women who stepped down from the carriage in the shadow of the ornate stately home.

Their initial task was to pull the dustsheets from the furnishings and throw open the shuttered windows to awaken the great, sleeping house. The previous owner had cut his live-in staff down to just two and as the Halifax women looked around, their footsteps echoing on the polished floors, they could see there was plenty of work to be done. The problem was a shortage of people to do it.

Mary Sherwood, described in the 1871 census as 'Head in Charge' was to act as housekeeper, and straight away she made a tour of the rooms, noting what she and the maid Ann Bedford would tackle first to keep their employers comfortable until more help arrived. For now the only other servant was Mary's teenage daughter who was to be the cook, but she would have to get her hands dirty too, if they were to have any hope of keeping on top of things. It wasn't long before the attic bedrooms began to fill with staff, many of them collected from the village, and Somerleyton Hall started to take on the appearance of a truly magnificent, well-ordered house once more.

Households of this stature had a double set of domestics. The upper tier were most likely to have direct contact with their employers and might include a butler, valet, housekeeper, cook and lady's maid. The lower echelon, who would be largely unseen and unheard by all but their colleagues, could consist of footmen, housemaids, maids of the kitchen, still-room, scullery, laundry and dairy, also coachmen, grooms, odd-job men and hall boys. Sir Francis and Lady Crossley would have involved themselves only in the selection of their personal helpers. Once the top tier were in place, the hiring and firing of the rest could be left in their hands. In those days most employees were taken on recommendation and the lack of employment law or unions meant that unsatisfactory staff were soon sent packing.

First on the Crossleys' shopping list was a butler and the job specification was demanding. He would need a good knowledge of wine, of dining room etiquette, of keeping silver gleaming and untarnished, and of keeping the footmen and hall boys in equally sparkling form. The butler was also in charge of the waiting at table, the lighting and heating of the labyrinth of rooms, and the valuables of the house. Not surprisingly, the advice of the day was to look for a man whose conduct was above suspicion and who would set a good example to all those below him. The Crossleys found just such a man.

Charles Howes, born in the nearby village of Belton in 1843, epitomised the popular view of an upright, smart and devoted manservant. At the age of 19 he was among the first servants to be taken on by the new owners of the hall and in the early days, Howes' job was quite straightforward, so he had plenty of time to learn as he went along. Sir Francis, with Cromwellian sympathies and little respect for those born into privilege, did not go in for lavish balls or 'hob-nobbing' with the rich and beautiful. He was blunt and he had little time for people who neither needed nor wanted to work. From the start Howes knew exactly where he stood: as long as he was loyal and diligent, there would be a job for him for life.

Howes received an annual salary of just over £65, which was about the average for country butlers at the time. A typical day consisted of tasks such as helping his master to dress, serving breakfast, sorting out the mail and paying bills. He cleaned the silverware and put it on show or set it out on the table in its perfect place, without a smudge. Charles also kept the key to another Aladdin's Cave - the wine cellar, with its racks of ruby port, amber whisky, and fine wines by the cask. In the coming years, Somerleyton would become a byword for hospitality.

When guests came to stay, Howes would arrange for them to be met at the station if they came by train, or he would have spruce boys ready to help them down from their carriages. He had footmen to valet the gentlemen if they came alone, and he took personal care of Sir Francis' clothes in the early days. After a ball or dinner party, Howes would wait up to see that the hall was secure after all the dining, drinking and talking were done.

That might not be until the early hours of the morning.

Although Howes lived out, he frequently slept at the hall. A makeshift, pull-down bed in the butler's pantry offered only a brief rest for his tired limbs, before the servants began rising again at 5.30 for the morning chores. With so few staff at first, Howes needed plenty of energy to keep up with the jangling of the servants' bells, but he did find time to socialise too. A new sewing maid had just come down from Halifax, and the charming, gentle butler found himself spending increasing amounts of time in her vicinity.

Charles married Elizabeth Smith and by 1872 the couple had their own family to think about. Just when they seemed settled there was a change of regime at the hall and Charles' life was to alter radically.

The death of Sir Francis Crossley was a blow to all concerned and his widow Martha then became estranged from her Halifax in-laws, so she retreated to Somerleyton virtually full-time. Initially her son Savile was away at university and by the time he came of age in 1878 he was making friends with some very influential people. He was earmarked for a career in politics and from the moment he entered the public arena, the responsibilities of his staff mounted as many VIP's came to visit Somerleyton, including members of the Royal family. This meant that Howes would see less and less of his own family.

Home for Charles Howes was a small cottage at Kitty's Farm, Ashby, on the Somerleyton Estate, where he lived with his wife Elizabeth. By 1881 they had five children, and Elizabeth's 70-year-old mother had moved from Halifax to share their home. Sadly, two of their children died in 1883. Child mortality was by no means uncommon, but that knowledge would have done little to ease the pain of their bereavement. He did find some comfort in his faith, as Charles was a regular supporter of the local chapel, walking down to the village every Sunday, a four-mile round trip. The Union Chapel regularly attended by Charles and his family was situated in the grounds of the hall until it was moved to a site in Somerleyton Street in 1882, when Sir Savile changed his allegiance and attended Church of England services instead. Charles remained firm in his Methodist beliefs.

By now there was little free time for Howes and even at the height of his career he could never be considered well off. Of course, there were 'perks';

*The Union Chapel in the Street — the ivy-clad house next door would become
home for successive butlers*

staff recalled that leftovers from sumptuous meals could be taken home as
treats. Hunks of ham, beef, venison or lamb would normally be beyond the
means of a butler's wage, and his family would have exclaimed with delight at
the delicacies made with chocolate, cream and exotic fruits. However, as a
strict teetotaller there was no question of Howes helping himself to the fine
wines he handled, even if they were leftovers. In some wealthy homes, butlers
were caught taking great quantities for themselves, but the problem never
arose at Somerleyton. His job did require him to taste the wines to check their
suitability, so somehow he managed to balance this with his religious beliefs.
Perhaps he took just a sip and spat it out. With a cask of good wine costing
over £20, he could be proud of his resistance to temptation.

In 1887 Sir Savile's marriage brought a glamorous new Lady Crossley
on to the scene, who was much in demand for social events and she made full
use of the hall's grand salons. She could dream up a costume ball of such
proportions that Somerleyton Hall would appear to have entered a time warp,
with historical characters lurking round every corner.

It was down to Howes to make sure these glittering events ran smoothly,
whether they were held in Suffolk or in London. The Crossleys now had a
mansion in fashionable Carlton House Terrace, overlooking the Mall, and the
family were frequently on the move between London in the Season and

Somerleyton out of it. With such a full schedule, Sir Savile had enlisted the services of a valet and Howes took a step back from the personal care of his employer, but he showed no offence. While other employees hopped from one job to another to find better money or status, Charles Howes was content to stay put.

In fact, the perceived status of a butler rose in line with that of his employer, so Charles could have been forgiven for adopting airs and graces as Sir Savile became more successful and respected in his own career. Instead, he is remembered as being a gentle, kindly soul who would pitch in and help wherever he could. Soon after the marriage of Sir Savile and Phyllis, the couple attended a celebratory dinner at Oulton Workhouse and it was Charles Howes who worked the projector to show slides of Somerleyton Hall and Estate to the inmates. Another time, he would be overseeing the entertainment of the King of England.

By the turn of the century, Charles was middle-aged. Talking about those days, Sir Savile's daughter Monica remembered their faithful butler as 'one of the old sort, with his neat whiskers and faultless black dinner-jacket suit. We all had a great respect for him. He knew where everything was in the house and we found it difficult to get on without him when he retired after 48 years.' He made that break in 1910.

Charles had immense pride in his own children, and his grandchildren. His daughter Alice had married a Welshman, William Evans the clerk at Somerleyton Estate, and Alice's children would not be destined to serve others.

The Evans family: William, left and Alice, centre with their seven children

Alice's son John would one day become Sir John Evans, deputy chairman of the board of the Inland Revenue, and her daughter Jennett was a Grammar School head teacher for 26 years. Jennett remembers her grandfather Charles Howes with great affection. 'I was born in 1908, just after the death of my grandmother. By the time I was of an age to register, Grandfather, or Taid as we called him, which is Welsh for Grandfather, had retired. He had a beard when I knew him, although I should doubt that it would have been permitted when he was working at the hall. Taid was a gentle, kindly man, I was very fond of him. As butler he would have had responsibility for other people, but he wouldn't ever have been sharp with anybody.'

Charles re-married and his second wife was the widowed Alice Cole, a former neighbour. Second marriages were not always greeted favourably in the village, even for widows, but Alice's choice of husband had the approval of her family, and the couple enjoyed 12 years of happy marriage.

Charles Howes died on March 8th 1922, aged 78. He was buried at Somerleyton alongside his first wife, and the tombstone reads, 'Life's race well run, Life's work well done, Life's battle won, Now comes rest.'

In that same year, Charles' stepson, Sam Cole, became butler at Somerleyton Hall.

Sam's arrival was in fact a return to Somerleyton, it was the village where he had been born and raised. He had served a difficult apprenticeship and his life had been punctuated by considerable tragedy, but he saw at the hall an opportunity for some degree of security following the trials of the Great War and the ensuing depression.

Sam was the son of a farm bailiff on the estate and he had been a childhood friend of Sir Savile's heir, Frank Crossley. They had enjoyed many a rough-and-tumble adventure together, much to his mother's consternation. Sam's father died in 1901 following an accident on the estate and in spite of compensation and a small pension, Mrs Cole struggled to make ends meet. Sam, a tall, hungry boy, was earning £14 a year doing farm work, and his income became vital. Next he was given a junior's gardening job, mainly washing flowerpots and running errands. Then during the shooting season, 15 year old Sam was asked by Howes the butler to help in the hall, and he found the work to his liking. He was taken on as a hall boy, the first rung on the domestic service ladder.

In his memoirs, Sam noted, 'I had to do the servants' hall meals for about a dozen people. These were footmen and housemaids; the stillroom maid and kitchen staff had their meals in the kitchen. Also I had to get meals for the butler and housekeeper and ladies' maid in the housekeeper's room, which was known as Pug's Parlour by the younger staff.' This nickname for the housekeeper's room was a traditional one; upper servants in large establishments were known as Pugs.

Sam was jogging along quite happily in his apprenticeship until his job satisfaction took a turn for the worse. He explained, 'When we went to London for the Season I found the work much harder. I had to fetch coal, scrub passages and worst of all, had to clean windows. Some of these were three and four storeys high. To clean the outside I had a belt round the waist with a chain each side which I had to fasten to hooks outside the window. I used to be terrified when the day came for window cleaning.'

As well as this Dickensian ritual, Sam was sent on errands around the bustling city, often becoming lost, and on one occasion he was nearly cajoled into joining the army. Haunted by the prospect of his hazardous window cleaning task, he took a job with the Earl of Ancaster's family as steward's room boy, which came with a smart livery suit and a pay rise to £24 a year with 3s.6d. a week beer money.

He bid a sad farewell to the Crossleys but, as well as stepping up a rung in terms of job title, he could now learn more about the intricacies of an upper domestic's work. The steward in charge, a kind of butler-cum-clerk, would teach him many a valuable lesson, and as he developed a critical eye for detail and strove to become a master of organisation, he would become, in the words of a former colleague, 'A Class Act'.

When war broke out in 1914 Sam enlisted in the Royal Sussex Regiment and, after a break to marry his sweetheart Jessie, he was sent to France where he served in the trenches at the Somme, potential fodder for cannons, snipers, and, just to exacerbate the anguish, lice. When he hung his rain-soaked coat on a bush to dry, it was blown to pieces. Drenched and now frozen, Sam became dangerously ill and was lucky to be found alive. Still on a stretcher, he arrived back at Norwich station at 2am one winter's morning where locals jostled to offer the wounded heroes cigarettes and chocolate. Sam remembered, 'I almost cried when one man came to me and said, "How are you a-doin' bor?" It was so good to hear the old familiar accent.'

In fact, Sam was never entirely well again. The war had left him with a weak heart. On a visit to his mother, he enquired about and was offered the vacant position as butler at Somerleyton Hall for Sir Savile and Phyllis, who were now Lord and Lady Somerleyton. The job was an attractive one, but after much discussion with Jessie, Sam turned it down. One day, though, he was offered a very strange interview.

A large car drew up outside the Coles' house and the chauffeur asked

Sam to come and speak to its occupant. Through the window, Lady Somerleyton asked Sam if he would help out with some shooting parties and other events. He agreed, and as each successful occasion came and went, Phyllis commented 'I hope you will soon be with us for good.' Finally, Sam and Jessie agreed.

Sam Cole (right) with footman William Beechener

The year was 1922. Lord Somerleyton was happy to take on a man of such good character as butler. As well as his distinguished service in peacetime, Sam Cole had proved himself in battle and that mattered a great deal with his Lordship. However, Jessie was less than keen to leave her town house with its running water, paved streets and shops nearby. At Somerleyton, there was mud everywhere, it was difficult to make friends, and she craved the stimulation of a library or newspaper service. The village had neither. After a year the family was offered a house in a better position, it was in the main street and close to Sam's mother. Called the Nook, it was a small semi-detached cottage with a pump in the yard and a copper for washing in the outhouse. Jessie had help in the house and a daily newspaper delivered by post. Sometimes she managed to get to Lowestoft and borrow books from the library. Things were looking up.

Jessie was a self-sufficient woman, a strange breed to the Somerleyton folk who, by their own admission, often had little ambition or cultural interest. She often felt frustrated at the downtrodden existence of her neighbours, but she helped to start up a branch of the Women's Institute and gradually she found a handful of like-minded ladies who brought respite to her loneliness. Lady Somerleyton would often take her shopping, but Jessie could only admire the fancy goods, and help carry her companion's boxes of purchases to the car.

The Coles had many privileges, such as permission to use a boat on the lake, or borrow a gun and shoot rabbits and ducks, and Sam's talents of organisation and discipline were much appreciated by his employers and their guests. Sometimes he could go home with tips of £5 or more. With his take-home salary being just £11 a month it was a fortune indeed, and one which he put aside for his children's education. His daughter Rowena adds, 'Yes, he enjoyed the job but my mother didn't enjoy him having it. She found it very difficult because he was occupied most evenings so she was alone a lot.' Worse still, Rowena says, 'After Christmas the family went to London and my father would go up there sometimes. He'd be away for quite a long time. When Lord Somerleyton was Lord in Waiting to King George V my father was away quite a bit and I can remember writing to him.'

Sam wrote in his memoirs about these trips, when he would accompany Sir Savile, now Lord Somerleyton, to Buckingham Palace or Windsor Castle. At the castle, he recalled, 'There was a formal dinner served at 9 o'clock to the head servants in a special dining room. Everyone had to wear evening clothes and assemble in the housekeeper's room. There, we were paired with a lady, and we walked into the dining room and took our places at the table, to be waited on by the junior servants, wearing livery. We were served with a four-course meal with appropriate wines, finishing with coffee and liqueurs. I did not often dine formally like this, as I found it rather boring.'

At home there were some welcome improvements.' 'Electricity came to the village,' said Sam, 'and it made life much easier. Out went the oil lamps and candles. An electric oven was installed in place of the old kitchen range and we bought an electric fire and a kettle'. Sam could adapt to just about anything, and dealing with people was his speciality. Savile's fortune had been dented during the War and he had become very watchful of expense. Woe betide the servant who made a habit of leaving lights on, or the guests who were too free with the postage stamps. On the other hand, Phyllis enjoyed her betting and entertaining, and fiercely resisted any attempts to make cutbacks in either.

With Savile's health causing problems, the younger Crossleys moved in too; Major Frank, Bridget his wife, and two children, Mary and William. Even at the age of seven, young Mary saw that her lively, modern-thinking family living under the same roof as the mercurial Lord and Lady Somerleyton was bound to cause tension at times. Frank and Bridget had their own circle of friends and hosted their own parties. Sir Savile would be sitting in the library and Lady Phyllis in her boudoir, each requiring attention. The staff needed to be very sharp-witted to please them all, and they were kept on their toes in this way for nearly five years.

Sam said, 'Then, in 1935, his Lordship and her Ladyship went on a cruise. One day, I received a telegram to say his Lordship had been taken ill and was in the ship's hospital. The ship would be landing at Tilbury and arrangements had been made to take him to a nursing home in London. I went to London and saw him installed in the hospital. Soon after, he had another stroke and died.' Major Frank Crossley became the second Lord Somerleyton and, said Sam, 'After a period of adjustment the household settled down into a pleasant routine. His Lordship and I resumed our boyhood friendship and had a free and easy relationship. It was good to be in a household with young children growing up and I became very fond of them indeed.'

In return, everyone was fond of 'Coley', especially the Crossley children. Bill, the third Lord Somerleyton, said, 'Sam Cole was a great character, he was always full of fun and was always joking. I remember when a new governess called Miss Vigers arrived, almost her first lunchtime he undid a ginger beer bottle behind her head and made a terrific pop rather like a champagne cork. Of course Miss Vigers absolutely jumped out of her skin, and we all roared with laughter. She didn't think it was a bit funny.'

Bill's sister Mary shared his love of the butler 'Coley', whom, she said, 'was a tremendous friend. We used to spend a lot of time in the pantry with him if we could. And he taught us all sorts - we used to have competitions, who could make the rudest noise, and the loudest, that sort of thing.'

A former kitchen maid remembers Sam Cole's love for the Crossley children, too, and how he used to let them ride around on his broom as if on a horse. He met his match with young nursery maid Violette Gunton, though, who said, 'One day I hid behind the wall by the stables and squirted him with a water pistol. He wasn't very happy. He boomed "Ugh! I was told only last week I could fall down any time, it's a wonder I don't fall down now!" Sam was referring to his poor heart condition, but he survived the ambush and continued living life to the full, both at work and at home.

Sam loved family life. His children called him 'Sammy' and took advantage of his soft nature whenever he was left in charge of them. An understanding man, he was concerned when Rowena was ribbed at Lowestoft High School about her father's job, with many jibes about 'what the butler saw'. Between them they agreed that he could be called Steward instead, at least to her friends. In fact, Rowena says that her father never indulged in gossip about his employers even though he was privy to their private conversations and habits. The family had a standing joke though, about the fact that Sam could never sit down to a meal without first adjusting the cutlery on the table, even the minutest fraction of an inch. His work was indeed his life.

Like others, Sam was deeply distressed when news came that Britain was about to be cast into another war, when he thought that his action in France had helped to put an end to all wars. His own son was sent out to fight in France, and with him went many of the village's young men. Once again there was a dearth of male help and in Somerleyton Hall Sam was seeing history repeated as, like Charles Howes before him, he was left to cope with several jobs at once. But Sam Cole was no agile young man. The Great War had broken his health and he knew that something would soon have to give. With great regret, he left Somerleyton once more and took up a job with Jarrold's department store in Norwich.

Sam Cole was a hard act to follow, but one of his successors was Wilfred Douglas who held the position for four years during the 1950s. Wilfred's father had been head horseman at Kitty Farm on Somerleyton Estate and young Wilf had started working in the hall stables at the age of 14. Later he came inside as pantry boy, and then he was quickly promoted to second footman, working under Cole the butler. Wilf was away during the war, serving in the RAF and when he came back he and his wife moved to Newmarket to look after the widowed Lady Somerleyton in her new home. She then went to London where she died soon after and Wilf returned to Somerleyton Hall as butler.

It was said that he was instrumental in the decision to open the hall to the public in 1956, although people had been coming to see the gardens for decades before that. He was polite and unassuming, but he kept a close eye on the streams of visitors who came to see the informal displays of Somerleyton treasures. There is a story that one lady complained that the 2s.6d. entrance fee was far too much for what was on view, so when she left Wilfred handed the money back to her with a ceremonious bow.

Wilf had enjoyed his time at Newmarket when he was working for the dowager Lady Somerleyton and he took the opportunity to return there in 1962 when he became house steward at the Jockey Club.

Now the days of truly servile domestics was coming to an end and the last man to take the chief manservant's role at Somerleyton was Jimmy Rumsby. Born Percy James Rumsby in 1915, Jimmy was the son of a Somerleyton gardener and he had started in the hall gardens himself. When he found himself in some difficulties, Lady Somerleyton took him under her wing and installed him in the house. Jimmy did all kinds of odd jobs, first working under the butler Wilfred Douglas and learning the art of silver polishing, valeting and waiting at table. Earning £9 a week in the post-war era, he ranked among the other general workers in the hall and on the estate, but was the natural successor when Douglas vacated the role of butler. Times had changed, though.

Jimmy, a shy bachelor, was as devoted to his job as any before him and he carried out most of the traditional butler's role, but there was already a decline in the Crossleys' socialising, and in their need for staff, so Jimmy had to be more of a Jack of all trades. He cleaned shoes - unheard of for a butler in Sam Cole's time — he was valet to Lord Somerleyton and he dealt with everything from washing up to polishing the silver. Ironically, as Jimmy's workload became increasingly varied, his status diminished. By the time he reluctantly retired in the 1980s he was known by some as the butler and by others simply as the 'Odd man'- a job description previously reserved for a lower domestic. Jimmy reluctantly retired in the 1980s and the position has not been filled full-time since his departure.

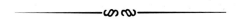

While the butler was at the top of the tree as far as the male servants were concerned, the housekeeper dominated the female staff outside of the kitchen. With a bunch of keys as badge of office, she wielded mighty power, ever watchful for unscrubbed corners or untidy maids, making sure that no dust, spider, mop or girl settled for too long.

The first housekeeper to serve the Crossleys at Somerleyton Hall was Mary Sherwood, a widow who had presided over their humbler mansion, Belle Vue in Halifax. Her daughter Elizabeth came down to Somerleyton to do the cooking, and the young girl caught the eye of the estate's agent, Kerry Rix. When they married, both Elizabeth and her mother gave up their life in service to live with him.

Martha Gurney, a spinster in her fifties from the nearby village of Lound, took over the housekeeping and moved into the hall with the growing team of maids. There were two women from Yorkshire, Mary Farrer then aged 49 and Sarah Savory, 26. Also Eliza Grint, 23, had come from Norfolk. A Somerleyton girl, Lydia Pope joined them and at 17 she no doubt took on the jobs that were hardest on the knees.

In 1877 Martha Gurney's wages amounted to around £25 a year, less than a London housekeeper might attract, but that was with food and lodging provided. As number two in rank, she, like the butler, had to be utterly trustworthy and a highly organised individual. She had to be accountant, diplomat and taskmaster all rolled into one and, as overseer of the female staff, she had to deal with the emotional ups and downs of the homesick and the lovelorn, as well as those who simply didn't get on with each other.

Besides her daily duties, Martha had a yearly cycle of tasks to delegate, according to the seasons. In winter there were fires to be lit and maintained, or the cavernous rooms at Somerleyton Hall would feel like draughty igloos. Muddy boots would mean a constant round of floor cleaning, and when shooting parties took place there would be guests needing maids to help with washing water, clothes and even childcare. In the spring the family would be away for the Season, mostly in London where they held and attended a series of parties and balls, and then the hall could be given a thorough clean from top to bottom. Estate workers were brought in to beat carpets and sweep chimneys and all the curtains and linens could be revived after the winter's accumulation of smoke, soot and dust.

When Martha retired, Emma Cory took over before becoming head of the Somerleyton laundry, and for 12 years Lily Giles was housekeeper to the Crossley family. In 1912 Sir Savile took on a cockney housekeeper, Emma Jaggard, who would remain with the family until she died.

Relief housekeeper Phyllis Lawn (centre) with maids

Emma Jaggard was everything a housekeeper should be, and more, but her personality remained cloaked in her reticence. In spite of her 50-year bond with the Crossleys, she kept strictly to the employer-servant relationship and divulged nothing of her past. Lady Crossley had taken it upon herself to chastise the guardians of one of her maids, an orphan who had been mistreated, but Emma would not let on what had happened to her own family, no matter how much Phyllis probed.

One former housemaid, Gertie Norton, who served under Emma in the 1930s described her as 'a lovely person, but she always seemed old. She wore a long dress and she always had a little round white net cap on her head.

Her hair was grey and she was a biggish person, plumpish. Dear old soul, she was. She was very good to me.'

Others did not like Emma so much and took exception to her blunt manner. Certainly, any girls who fell short of her ideals were given a taste of her wrath. 'She used to get on at some of them what wouldn't work', said Gertie. 'She'd shout at them. Some of them were lazy, some got stood off.'

Ironically, those who remember Emma Jaggard cannot recall what she actually did all day. A former charlady at the hall said, 'I don't know what ever she used to do, only give orders. You'd never see her working. But the other girls had to be on their guard.' There is no suggestion she was idle, though. Gertie insists, 'She was devoted to the family. She never went out and she never took a rest. She'd tell us to go and rest in the afternoon and said she did, but whenever we'd come down she was there.'

A housekeeper's role was to see that work was done, not to do it herself. So Emma would have been constantly touring, some might suggest prowling, round all the rooms to check that everything was in place and nothing could offend the eye of the highly observant master and mistress. There should be soap, water, towels, lamps, writing paper and ink in the bedrooms when required, especially for guests, and downstairs there was a snow-capped mountain of linen to manage, ranging from fine damask napkins for the Crossleys' dining room to industrial quality towels for drying the rough hands of the domestics. There were cloths for glass, dusters for china, and, just in case a speck of dirt should suddenly materialise, footmen kept a pocket-sized cloth to deal swiftly with the offending particle.

Emma's wages varied according to whether or not they included her food - when the family were away she would be on 'board wages', with extra money for living expenses. Typically she was paid £4 2s 10d a month, which rose to £4 4s for board wages. At around £50 a year, this was a good wage for a housekeeper. Her senior housemaid, Marjorie Balls, was paid just over half that salary, and a maid like Gertie Norton received just 'five bob a week', or £13 a year.

Emma kept her own counsel and revealed little about herself. She ducked any direct questions, and even, or perhaps especially, kept her employers at arm's length. The Honourable Mrs Mary Birkbeck, sister of the third Lord Somerleyton, recalls, 'She was definitely born and bred in London, and she had a Cockney accent. I remember her telling me that she joined the family in London. Apparently she had started work as a nurserymaid somewhere at the age of 12. As far as I know she had no relations, but I have no idea - I was a small child and as such one would not have asked - and later on she was part of the establishment to such an extent that the question never arose. Her bedroom was her home, it was barred to us, though after I married and she had retired I did go and visit her when I was at Somerleyton. We were all frightened of her. She appeared fierce and austere though no doubt had a heart of gold and was of course loyalty itself. I never remember her having a holiday.'

The only known photograph of Emma Jaggard

Mary's mother Bridget became Lady Somerleyton in 1935 and, says Mary, 'I know she too was scared of Emma and I think remained so, like the rest of us! I never remember Emma laughing though she had a nice smile, but she was always gloomy. When I introduced my future husband to her, her only comment was "Think well before you do it!" and when wedding presents arrived in quantity and she was helping me clear up paper, I laughingly reminded her that when my brothers got married, the parcels would mostly go to future brides' homes, so clearing up would be lessened; Emma's remark was, "You never know, them poor girls may never 'ave no 'omes"! '

Mary continues, 'Our wedding was in London in 1950 and Emma declined to come. After we were married and staying at Somerleyton, she always insisted on 'calling' us in the morning with early tea and brown bread and butter as she always did all visitors except those who brought their own lady's maids. She would knock, come in and draw the curtains, saying, "Mornin' Miss, Mornin' Sir" in a very gloomy voice, before withdrawing with a comment about the weather.'

Emma's sombre mood extended to her clothing, and she mostly wore black dresses, says Mary. 'She always looked rather upholstered but when she got old she got very thin and small.' Even then Emma simply refused to retire from the service of the Crossley family. Staff remember that she cried and begged to stay, so her bedroom became her retirement home, and with difficulty she was gradually relieved of her duties. Everyone, even Lady Bridget, took part in caring for Emma, but still they couldn't prise out any information about any surviving relatives, and nobody came to visit her. As her strength waned, Emma sent girls out every spring to collect snowdrops and tie them in bunches. Nobody recalls to whom they were sent. Finally, she had to leave Somerleyton Hall. In her 94th year, she was admitted to hospital in Great Yarmouth. Her stay was short.

One of her colleagues, Harry Wilson, wrote the following obituary in April 1962: 'From a mansion in London to a large country house, ruling her department in her own way, and not taking kindly to any interference, Emma served the family for a longer time than is given to most of us. It fell ill with anybody who fell short of her standards, whether employer or her staff, they were left in no doubt as to her opinions. But behind the outward manner shown to the world was a kind and generous heart to man, animals and birds. Many received a helping hand from her.'

'At Carlton House Terrace, a stately London mansion, she greeted me with a few instructions as to her expectations of me. After the First World War, owing to changed conditions she quickly adapted herself to a smaller staff and establishment. But seemingly she found more time to correct our shortcomings and also to visit with us some of London's places of interest, which she loved so well. She often called us at 4 o'clock in the morning and when asked why she got up so early she would reply "I shall get up what time I like." I can picture her now, coming into the dining room after dinner to see if we had brushed any crumbs off the table on to the carpet and casting a critical eye even on the dignified butler whose remarks were certainly not dignified!'

'Then came the change to country life at Somerleyton. Taking it all in her stride she carried on in her persistence of duty. As advancing years curtailed some of her activities she still made her will known and disliked leaving to others what she considered her duties. When time and age took their toll she had to take to her bed and was cared for by those she had served so long.'

'The changes in the past 50 years she sometimes found difficult to accept. But at Somerleyton she was understood and not 'put out of her ways'. In the eventide of life it was HOME. Of one thing I am certain, as one who has known her for many years, that she will be remembered as one of the outstanding personalities when most of us are forgotten. Perhaps that may be a measure of success in life, overlooking human failings and deserving of that well known epitaph, "Well done, good and faithful servant, Enter thou into the joy of the Lord."'

A tribute to Emma Jaggard was erected in Somerleyton Church, and Emma's body lies at rest near to her beloved Crossley family. When her room was cleared, staff found just a few old photos, presumably they were her family. Nobody knows for sure.

There could never be another Emma Jaggard, and although the Crossleys have employed other housekeepers, the terms of reference have changed considerably. There is no army of maids to keep in check; electrical appliances are the weapons against dust these days. Cleaners still have to be thorough, of course, and anyone who dares to take shortcuts in their work might well feel a sudden chill of disapproval from Emma, still cited by many as The Housekeeper of Somerleyton Hall.

Below stairs, the triumvirate of power at the hall consisted of the butler, the housekeeper and finally the cook. Each of them could make or break the social reputation of the family, and as time went on, the Crossleys demanded nothing but the best. In the early years, though, they were much more relaxed about their food.

Sir Francis and Lady Crossley did not have cosmopolitan tastes. Their teenage cook, Elizabeth Sherwood, could rely on her basic skills, making recipes out of the staple ingredients she was given. Typical entries in the hall's accounts show purchases of meat, fish, dairy produce, and groceries, mostly from local suppliers. Only after Sir Savile became master of the house did the shopping list change. Oysters appeared, and two casks of wine costing £44. Five gallons of whisky were bought for £7 5s. The home farm produced all the meat and vegetables they could need, and in addition the tropical glasshouses glistened with figs, grapes and peaches.

At this time Elizabeth Sherwood left to marry the estate agent and a succession of cooks came and went in the next decade. By the turn of the century, the curriculum vitae of a Somerleyton cook had to be as impressive as the multi-course menus that Sir Savile's gourmet guests expected to enjoy. Of course, cooking was a skill that every working-class girl learned, but for it to become their profession they had to turn their hand to more than the general fill-up fare of stews and puddings. They could have a whole world of ingredients at their fingertips, if they knew how to make a meal of them.

There was no special training school for the girls, so they usually started as kitchen maids and worked their way up. Sometimes the cook in charge was generous with advice, others guarded their tricks of the trade jealously. At Somerleyton, one relief cook was brought in especially for her skill at baking bread and buns. It was an exacting science, as her descendant, Graham Richmond, explains. 'Phyllis Baxter used to bake her bread in the old brick oven at the hall. That was lit early in the morning with a faggot of wood and when all the wood had burned away, the oven was hot enough. The ash was brushed from the stone slab at the bottom, and Phyllis would put her hand in to feel the temperature, then in went the bread. You got the fierce heat to start with, then that gradually cooled down and that was ideal as the loaf finished.'

There were few gadgets or labour-saving devices, every ingredient was prepared by hand and virtually nothing was wasted. Bones, vegetable peelings, even eggshells all went into the giant stock-pot which bubbled constantly on the range, while rabbit skins were sold to the local tradesman and dripping was a perk for the cook to sell.

Everything was freshly dug, picked, killed or delivered, and for a new kitchen maid, some of the items had only been seen before in dreams. But that's not to say that young would-be cooks were always envious, as one trainee of that era, Kate Chapman recalled in the East Anglian magazine. 'My first job was to skin a hare for roasting. It was very 'high' and had an awful smell and was full of maggots. After skinning it I was pumping water on to it to get rid of the maggots and blood when cook came running towards me shouting: "What are you doing? I want that blood for a pudding." I thought, "If that is the sort of thing they eat here I don't think I'm going to like it". I liked it even less when I saw some of the maggots in the gravy.'

The girl's mouth did water when she had to peel and pip fruit for dessert, but the pears, grapes, plums and pineapples were not to pass her lips until they had been passed around the dinner table first.

The job held some rewards; a good cook had considerable freedom in her own domain, and even the butler had no jurisdiction in the kitchen. During periods of frenetic activity, no-one would wish to be in the midst of it all unless they had to be, but the lull after the storm was bliss, and the kitchen staff could enjoy the fruits of their labour if supply exceeded appetite in the dining room. Considering the quantity of rich leftovers that could come their way, it is no wonder that many cooks were caricatured as portly, rosy-faced creatures.

Cooks were often strong characters, and they needed to be. Dinners could easily run to six courses or more, with state occasions requiring perhaps a dozen dishes, with hors d'oeuvres, soups, fish, choices of entrees, meat, game, sweets and savouries. There would be no simple meat-and-veg options, and it was down to the cook to organise her kitchen maids so that everything was on hand for her to create her masterpieces and have them at the right temperature and in the right order for the fastidious diners. There was no time for replacing spoiled sauces or floppy soufflés, and the ultimate shame for a cook would be to have a dish returned as unsuitable. Skill in salvaging a meal from the jaws of disaster was all part of a cook's knowledge. Each day's menu was scrutinised by the lady of the house, so it took great cunning and flair to cover up mishaps mid-recipe. However, it was one thing to attract criticism from the family, but quite another to leave the King of England in want of his lunch. That could so easily have happened had it not been for the iron nerve and smart moving Somerleyton cook, Mrs Harman.

Mrs Harman said she had a very happy life at the hall, starting as second kitchen maid in 1909 when she was aged 22. She quickly graduated to first kitchen maid and then to cook. By 1912 she had proved her skill at providing sumptuous meals for any occasion, including visits by King George V and Queen Mary. In July of that year their Majesties toured Halifax and the Crossleys' carpet mills, so when they stopped for lunch at the home of one of the family, no other cook would do but Mrs Harman. She travelled North from Somerleyton especially to prepare the meal herself.

Such was the character of Mrs Harman that her action was recorded in the 'Royal Tour' supplement to the Halifax Guardian newspaper of the time. Under the heading Cooking for the King it stated, 'All the cooking for the luncheon was done by Lady Crossley's cook. Whilst at Somerleyton she has often cooked the food when the King and Queen have been entertained and she was determined to do the whole of the preparation on this occasion, and resolutely refused offers of assistance with an almost humorous emphasis. The King and Queen know her cooking, she declared, and they should know it today. The greater portion of the viands came from Somerleyton, and the wines were also from the cellars of that beautiful residence. In addition to an army of smoothly-working female servants, it was necessary to have no fewer than 15 footmen to wait at the tables. Five of these were staff at Somerleyton and the remainder from London.'

The reporter was allowed to look into the room after the guests had vacated, and he wrote in glowing terms about the lavish setting for the meal, at which 28 people were entertained, with Sir Savile and Lady Phyllis taking prime positions next to the monarchs. Behind the scenes, all had not run quite as smoothly as it seemed. Mrs Harman herself described the moment of horror when she found that her carefully prepared food had been filched.

'It was on an occasion when Sir Savile and Lady Phyllis were in Halifax to show King George V over the carpet mill. I was asked to prepare lunch for the party; fried sole and a grilled cutlet. The food was ready and waiting while the royal party had their photographs taken, but then the food began to disappear from the table - the servants were helping themselves! So preparations had to be made all over again with the greatest speed, and we managed to make good the loss.'

Like many others, Mrs Harman had to adapt to changing times and there were great contrasts in her experiences. From royal lunches to tea for inmates of the workhouse, she could cater for any palate and any number, which was just as well in the days of the Great War. She said, 'During the First World War, when Lady Phyllis opened up the billiard room for wounded sailors and then much of the rest of the hall for more wounded service men, the park was full of army camps. Every Tuesday and Friday the older folk from the village went up to the hall for soup at about 12 noon. There was pea soup on Tuesdays and barley soup on Fridays, with a general preference for the latter.' The hall gardens supplied produce to the Cheshire Yeomanry while they were stationed in the grounds, but at least Mrs Harman did not have to cook for them. Meals for invalids, nurses, visitors and family were quite enough to contend with.

When Mrs Harman moved on to Dupplin Castle in Perth, her place was taken by another formidable lady, who, although unmarried, was known by the customary 'Mrs'- Mrs Pitman. She too was queen of her kitchen - so much so that even the Crossley children were frightened of her. Mary recalled, 'We weren't allowed in the kitchen, because Mrs Pitman was very fierce and she used to say "Get out of my kitchen" if we went anywhere near her. My mother used to go down there to order the meals, but my mother until the day she died couldn't really boil an egg, so how she knew how to order all this wonderful food, I don't know. Sometimes Mrs Pitman could be quite nice, I think, but give her her due, I expect she was fierce when she was cooking meals, and getting irritated, and hot and worried. Because she had so many meals to cook - there were four lots of food. There was food for the dining room, food for the housekeeper's room, and for the servants' hall, and food for the nursery. I think the nursery probably got fourth pickings.'

After Mrs Pitman, there was a succession of cooks at the hall. One is best remembered for her liking for beer, and former colleagues recall with some amusement her hit-and-miss efforts to contend with the agreed menu while under the influence. Mary Birkbeck tells how the cook came staggering off the train at Somerleyton one day to find that, instead of a chauffeur, Lady Somerleyton herself had come to meet her and she declared, 'What? Are yer keepin' a dog and barkin' yerself?' The woman had to go.

A later candidate, Rose Enticknap, was more suited to the job. The wife of Jack Enticknap the groom, she did not live at the hall like her predecessors, but came in daily from her home in the village. That she was devoted to the family is beyond question; she named one of her sons Francis Savile Crossley Enticknap. Rose was a one-woman team, with new gadgets as her maids and electricity bringing more control to the whole cooking process.

She was a dab hand at rabbit pies and melt-in-the-mouth cakes, both of which Lord Somerleyton was very keen on, but many of her skills would not be tested, for the new breed of Crossleys had no taste for enormous banquets.

The great kitchen range was pulled out in the 1960s, the old kitchen itself became a playroom, and a smaller, well-equipped one was installed for the family's modest needs. Rose Enticknap was again succeeded by a number of cooks, but the latest, Mrs Jill Howard, has served the Somerleyton family for 15 years. She has no need to yell at children or scold maids. Against a background hum, whirr and bleep of machinery she goes about her work, producing meals in a way which her predecessors might have thought was magic.

Rose Enticknap with husband Jack

Chapter 5

Doing the Dirty Work

The upper domestics undoubtedly held positions of great trust at Somerleyton Hall, cruising the corridors and wielding their power in their small kingdoms. They had a high degree of respect and status, but there were others who held the Crossleys' closest secrets and dearest treasures. They were the personal attendants; the lady's maid and the valet, and perhaps most important of all, the nursery staff and governesses.

This group often found themselves in a kind of limbo. They were not really lower domestics, so couldn't mix easily in the servants' hall and yet they were still domestics, not part of the family. They knew the most intimate details of the Crossleys' private lives but at no time would they divulge that knowledge or pass on gossip. Whatever generation they cared for, they were devoted to their charges.

When the Crossleys arrived in 1863 Sir Francis and Lady Martha did not have a specific valet and lady's maid, they had a sewing maid, Elizabeth Smith, to take care of dressmaking and repairs, while Charles Howes the butler attended to his master's needs. When the two attendants married, Elizabeth left and another Yorkshire woman, Mary Sutcliffe, came as a live-in lady's maid. Her salary for the year 1875 is recorded as just £14, with food and board provided. Mary Sutcliffe's duties revolved around the well-being and fine appearance of her employer. She needed to know the characteristics of every kind of fabric, how to mend it, clean it and put it away carefully, safe from moths and mustiness. She might have to re-curl feathers, soften leather, and iron the most delicate materials. She had to be able to select the right clothes for an occasion, and be sure they still fitted from one banquet to the next.

The lady's maid was expected to always display patience and willingness to oblige, even if that meant pandering to whims. In fact Lady Martha Crossley was far from whimsical, and not an ardent follower of fashion. That was made apparent when her son Savile married, and the newspapers ran out of adjectives to describe the outfits of the bride and her mother, while the groom's mother was passed off with the observation 'Lady Crossley came in terracotta velvet.'

Martha was a widow by then, and she soon moved out of the hall to make way for the newlyweds. When the new Lady Crossley sailed into the Somerleyton spotlight, the atmosphere changed. Phyllis owed nothing to humble family roots, she had been raised in comfort in a society where servants were treated as lesser mortals and certainly not as friends. Her critical eye for detail, coupled with a slashingly sharp tongue, could bring a weak disposition to despair, but she never failed to enlist and keep attendants who were loyalty incarnate.

One such lady was Miss Hudson, a small, obliging woman who suited her mistress in every sense. Phyllis started each day with a pungent bath scented with rose geraniums, after which she needed to do no more than hold out her arms to have a beautiful costume whispered onto her willowy frame. Her hair was then piled into a delicate sculpture and her appearance topped off with an abundance of accessories. Phyllis had a passion for jewels, and Miss Hudson took care of them, poking the dirt and powder from every crevice after use. With delicate attention she polished the handfuls of gold and diamonds, buffing their facets until their brilliant beauty matched that of their owner, leaving them winking and shining in the light. On other occasions when she was not attending to her mistress directly, Miss Hudson was closeted away, concocting all manner of potions and pastes to revive hats, shoes, gloves and magnificent dresses.

A cartoon from 1898 shows Phyllis at a shoot with Sir Savile, and describes her as 'a tall, pretty woman with bright golden hair and blue eyes, looking very well in black with white fur and a mauve hat with green plumes.' Many other reports indicate that she liked to be where the action was, so Miss Hudson also had to contend with the dust and mud that collected on her mistress' swishing long skirts and dainty boots. Other enemies included wax, which tended to drop from chandeliers, and ash from Phyllis' cigarettes. Then there was ink that would escape from pens, as well as the day-to day stains from perspiration and cosmetics, which were used liberally by her Ladyship.

The Crossleys travelled a great deal and their personal servants always followed. While Lady Crossley was enjoying the fresh air on a cruise or attending a society ball either at home or abroad, her maid would be confined to her own room much of the time. Even though she ate with the upper domestics she had little conversation to offer, in case she inadvertently gave away a snippet of gossip. Similarly she could not be taken into the confidence of any other servants, who sometimes held the belief that there was a spy among them. It is no surprise that one family member described the relationship between Phyllis and her lady's maid as being 'rather like a grand dog with a little spaniel at her heels.'

However, the mood changed dramatically when Bridget took the title of Lady Somerleyton. The new generation of Crossleys were, in common with the times, more sympathetic towards their staff and more inclined to treat them with humanity. Then, in the 1930s, fewer women were prepared to go into service and act the see-nothing, hear-nothing role, they were becoming choosier about their employment terms. But Bridget was a much warmer, more benevolent character than her mother-in-law, so she had no trouble recruiting lady's maids, and keeping them. Her first, Ivy Day, was assisting her before her marriage and even went on honeymoon with her mistress when Bridget first became Mrs Crossley.

When female guests came to stay at Somerleyton they often brought their own maid to attend on them, but those who did not were serviced by stand-ins from the household staff. The maids might sometimes find it tricky to please their temporary mistress, and one recalls that tips were rare. Looked at from the other side, the guests themselves might have had misgivings, too. Lesley Lewis, brought up in a large middle-class family in the first part of the century, described her dilemma in her book The Private Life of a Country House 1912-39, 'It was thought essential to have proper equipment of matching brushes to be set out on the dressing table. We were usually packed or unpacked for, and clothes were laid out on the bed before dinner. Should you wear without question what a strange housemaid had selected? Did she or did you know best and if you felt she did not, would she be hurt if you substituted something else? Did your underwear come up to scratch and was there enough of it?....Maids had a kindly but devastating way of taking shoes away to be cleaned or clothes to be dried and ironed, but if they did not bring them back in time should you ring or keep everyone waiting?' It could be a delicate relationship all round.

The male counterpart of the lady's maid was the valet, who had similar duties in taking care of his master's clothes, of his bathing needs and his hair potions, but he had the added responsibility of facial hair to deal with too. In the early days Savile sported a moustache, not an eccentric one, but it needed regular trimming and he could not be expected to do it himself. He was a smart dresser; photographs from 1930 show him in natty turned-up tweed trousers and black-and-white spats, but he also had old favourites in the wardrobe for pottering in the parkland and tending his beloved rhododendron shrubs. More than once he was mistaken for a gardener.

The valet had to go everywhere with Sir Savile, he had to pack his cases, make the travel arrangements, and dispense tips from a cash float he carried. His loyalty cannot be faulted when he was even prepared to go to war at his master's side and this certainly happened when Sir Savile went out to the Boer War in South Africa, where his Man was infected by typhoid into the bargain.

During the First World War, Savile was sent to France with the Red Cross and his life was made more comfortable there by his valet, or batman. One acquaintance who stopped on a route march to borrow Sir Savile's bathroom and shaving facilities also had a helper. He wrote in his diary, 'Then a washing clothes parade was much needed, and my bed was aired, also much needed. Changed my drawers for Scott to wash (lucky Scott!!)...then went down to town to buy provisions and dine.' Nothing was sacred between employer and hapless employee in these situations.

The Somerleyton valets were often kept apart from their colleagues, partly because of their code of secrecy but more because their long hours at work conspired to keep them from socialising. In turn their expectations were far above those of the general staff. Sir Savile's daughter Monica wrote, 'Garner was Dad's valet, a great character. He left in a huff when Dad didn't take him for a shooting trip to India and soon afterwards he became valet to Prince Arthur of Connaught but we never lost touch with him.' In that short description Monica confirms the theory that in later years a good personal manservant could almost write his own job specification, making demands that others would never dare try.

One former valet who had several widely differing jobs at Somerleyton was Harry Wilson. Born at the turn of the century, Harry was one of three brothers whose above-average intelligence was recognised but sadly underused, mainly because as working class boys they had no chance of a higher education or an executive career. So Harry, Jack and Egremont, or Egre for short, went to work on the estate when they were 14 and made the best of their time there. For each of them, that would lead to over 50 years' service of the Crossley family.

Harry was brought into the house to act as footman when needed and he often recounted the story of how, on one occasion, he had to stay up until 2 o'clock in the morning while the family played cards, so that he could switch off the lights when they had finished. It was unthinkable that they should do it themselves. But Harry's dedication was rewarded when he was made valet to Savile, the first Lord Somerleyton, at the age of 17.

Harry saw the heyday of his work as being when he travelled far and wide with Savile who was then Lord in Waiting to King George V, and the tall, smart valet mixed easily with prominent people and servants alike. When that great era came to an end, Harry found he had many other skills to fall back on. His high standard of workmanship especially at carpentry meant he could create masterpieces in wood. Promoted to estate foreman, he would take his orders every day from the agent, and he saw to it that his workforce kept the hall and grounds in immaculate order. His honesty and diplomacy also came in useful for dealing with tenants, and he would cycle round Somerleyton collecting rents come rain or shine, noting down their requests for repairs in his 'little black book'.

During World War II Harry helped tend the wounded soldiers in the hall's grand rooms where once he had waited on lords and ladies. He had a kind and generous nature, but he could be 'devastatingly critical' according to one colleague, and perhaps that partly explains why he never seemed to find the time or inclination to marry.

In his later years Harry lived with his sister Lucy in a tied cottage on the Green, and speaking to a journalist in 1976 he commented, 'I don't have to pay rent now, but I like to pay a pound a week. I think if you have a beautiful home with a lovely green through your window, you should be happy to pay.' The journalist could hardly believe he was being serious. But when asked about his hard days in service Harry snorted at the suggestion that staff were treated unfairly, especially at Somerleyton. He argued, 'Through two world wars the servants were fed like kings. People say service is a terrible thing, but we were all so happy.' Harry would never even think about the opportunities he might have had in more enlightened times. By the time of his death at the age of 80, it could truly be said that Harry had given his life to the service of the Crossley family and Somerleyton Hall.

Even when the family still employed a host of personal helpers, there were times when the faithful valet was not by his master's side. In such cases Frank Crossley was happy to call upon others to take on those tiresome jobs instead. Some seventy years later, still bemused by her experience, former nursery maid Violette Beechener, nicknamed 'Oddy', said, 'We used to go every year to London for a month, and the seaside for a month. The chauffeurs used to take the children and luggage in one car and I had to ride behind with Major Frank. Going along, he'd want a smoke and he'd say 'Fill my pipe, Oddy'. I'd never filled a pipe before! I'd seen my father do it, so I had to fill this pipe. And he said, 'Why, you've done it well'.

Violette herself worked in this kind of no-man's land within the domestic hierarchy. Like the personal attendants, the nursery staff were too close to the family to be entirely trusted by their serving colleagues, and yet they were still servants who had to remember their place, several notches down the social scale to their employers. Their job was perhaps the most important of all. Responsible for the welfare of the babies and growing young masters and mistresses, they held the future of the Crossley line quite literally in their hands.

At the turn of the century, Sir Savile's children had a nanny and nurserymaid who went everywhere with them, and his daughter Monica loved their Nanny Hilditch, who kept the children clean and presentable, tucked them up in bed at night and nursed them when they were ill. Nanny Hilditch had responsibility for all the cleaning, laundry and meals in the nursery, and that could often cause friction when her work overlapped with that of the housemaids, or the cook. To Nanny Hilditch, her charges came first, but to Cook, it was the older Crossleys who paid her wages and therefore had to be her first priority. At Somerleyton, the nursery was on the top floor, near to the servants' rooms, and the nimble young nursery maid was the one who had to descend two long flights of stairs to peer in at the kitchen hatch and take her trays of food, which then had to be carried back up to the summit.

When the next generation came to share Somerleyton Hall with Lord and Lady Somerleyton, Frank and Bridget brought their children and nursery staff too. Violette, or 'Oddy', was with them and she recalls that at first the incoming staff found it hard to fit in as denizens of the servants' landing. The nursery, on the same floor as the maids' bedrooms, came under critical eyes. 'I had to be very careful of the head housekeeper there, I'll tell you. I wasn't allowed to use my Ewbank sweeper, you know, I had to use a broom to sweep the long Day Nursery.' The fearsome housekeeper, Emma Jaggard, would brook no introduction of new-fangled devices. Labour was not for saving, it was for using, and she did not want her girls thinking that there might be an easier way to do things.

It was not only the nursery staff who fell foul of the Somerleyton maids at times. Frank and Bridget's daughter Mary was seven when she was put in a bedroom of her own. She said, 'All those bedrooms have got little peepholes at the top of the door. I was an avid reader and I used to read under the bedclothes with a torch, and of course Emma, then head housemaid and the dragon of the household, kept a beady eye on everybody. All the staff had to get up by half past five in the morning and if they saw my light on they used to always tell tales and I always got into terrible trouble if I was caught reading in the early morning.'

The nursery, like a great nest at the top of the house, was where the children ate, slept and played. They went out walking and riding, they had lessons in their schoolroom, and they were taken down to see their parents for an hour before bedtime, but otherwise they were self-contained. Mary describes the scene, 'There was a large room which was known as the day nursery and we couldn't see out of the windows because they were so high, but my father had a sort of balcony built with little steps up to it so we could all look out, which was a great pleasure to us. Then there was the night nursery, which was where Nanny slept with the youngest.'

Her brother Bill, Lord Somerleyton adds, 'I took my first bedroom when I was about eight. I remember being terrified, having left the night nursery, and I remember creeping along the passage and listening under the door of the nursery where Nanny was knitting in the evening. I had to make sure that somebody was there.'

In fact, somebody was always there. The nursery staff had no separate living space, their duties were completely bound up with the children, day and night. 'Oddy', had no complaints though. 'I've always liked to look after children, it was all I wanted to do. I didn't have my own room, I was in the nursery, you see. I slept with the older ones and Nanny had the babies. The nursery was my home. I think I must have had a wardrobe or something, but you didn't have many clothes or anything.'

Violette was with the family for six years, starting in 1927 at the age of 16. She had a good relationship with the nannies, of which there were several. The children loved their nannies too, in varying degrees. Mary said, 'I had a nanny called Nanny Ward to whom I was devoted, but she had to leave because her mother was ill. When my brother Bill was born he had a nanny called Nanny Mewett, who idolised him, but she was not so keen about me by any means. I remember when he got a little older I was locked in the bathroom to eat my rhubarb and rice pudding, but he always got more than me if there was something exciting, like strawberries. But I never held it against him! Then after my younger brother Nick was born, Nanny Mewett left because she couldn't bear the idea of another baby coming and superseding Bill. We then had a rather prim nanny, Nanny Peckham to whom we were all devoted, but she was quite heavy with the hair brush - she used to wield it with quite some force if she was annoyed.'

Violette Beechener, 'Oddy' with Mary and Bill

Violette has memories of those characters too. 'Everyone loved Nanny Ward, the Crossleys thought the world of her. Then there was Nanny Mewett. She was all right, but I think she left when Nicky came along because she didn't want to take on a third child. Then it was Nanny Peckham. She was a posh nanny. She used to call the butler 'Cole', and he used to get so cross. She used to drink her tea with her little finger held up and if Major Frank came up when we were having tea, he looked at me and used to mimic her. That started me giggling!'

Violette's day started at 6.30 am, when she would get up and take Nanny a cup of tea in bed, before cleaning the nursery and going downstairs to collect the children's cooked breakfast. There would be more cleaning, making of beds, washing, ironing and mending to do while the children were out either with Nanny or the governess. Mary Birkbeck adds that another ritual often took place. 'In my grandfather's time, when my parents went abroad, Nanny

Mewett, who my grandfather always called Nurse, took us downstairs at 9 o' clock while he was having his breakfast alone. He would make us walk round the table first, once, then run round the table to make sure we were fit. Rather as if we were young horses. And then we were sent back to the nursery.'

Mary's keen young senses also picked up the air of animosity between her guardians. 'There was always a tremendous atmosphere between the nanny and governess, they were jealous of each other. My elder brother Bill and I would be taken for walks in the garden or in the village with our governess, and if we met our younger brother Nick having a walk out in the pram with Nanny we were not allowed to talk to them.'

Nanny Ward with Nick

Violette had few problems getting along with the other domestics. She played tricks on the stately butler Sam Cole, and cheeked the footmen. One of them, William Beechener, would become her husband. Their time for courting was limited, as she only had a half-day a week free, and sometimes Sundays, once her work was done. Violette's pay was £36 a year plus food and lodging, and somehow she managed to save up for a bicycle, a great source of pride, and on which she travelled for miles around Suffolk and Norfolk.

Violette's spirit for adventure stood her in good stead when it came to testing out the new fire escape at Somerleyton Hall. She explains, 'They used to have chutes, covered in. I never went in one but the girls used to say they scraped their knees. The rope was the modern thing - they'd just put a belt round your middle and lower you out the window and down you had to go. You had to push away from the wall, or you'd smash yourself. That was in the maids' bedrooms, on the top floor. We had to practise, I was supposed to be one of the best ones at it, so Captain Flatt, the agent, said.' It was an undignified descent, and hard to believe that some of the more robust nannies would have gladly gone out the window, even in the most dire circumstances. Violette's uniform of a white frock and apron would not have lent itself to modesty in such cases, either.

Youth was an obstacle for Violette when it came to promotion, so she left the Crossleys to fulfil her ambition of becoming a nanny. In 1938 she married William Beechener and raised a family of her own, including a daughter, who she named Mary after her little charge at Somerleyton.

The Crossleys look back with affection to their nursery days, but the other member of the child-rearing team, the governess, was treated to a less than warm welcome. Lord Somerleyton recalls, 'Miss Vigers arrived one autumn, and we took her into the middle of the maze and then we ran out and left her there. When we got back my mother was furious - she said, "Where's Miss Vigers? What have you done with her?" and we said we'd left her in the middle of the maze. She was furious, she sent us back for her. When we went back, Miss Vigers was absolutely shaking with fear. And we thought of course she would leave us then, having had that sort of introduction to the Crossley family, but not a bit of it, she was with us for several years, and a very good governess.'

His Lordship's sister Mary takes up the tale, 'Poor Miss Vigers had a very rough time. She came to prepare my brother for Prep school and she came when I was seven. I don't think she'd ever taught a girl before. I think she'd always worked with little boys, they had to learn to read and write and the

Miss Vigers with Bill

rudiments of Latin and arithmetic. She was with us for four years and there's a room at Somerleyton which my brothers and I still think smells of Miss Vigers. She had a particular smell, it could have been a certain perfume. She ruled the roost in the schoolroom and she taught us a great deal, she must have been a wonderful teacher. One of the things I'm eternally grateful to her for is the wonderful books she used to read to us, and the books she made us read; Kipling, Thomas Hardy and other children's classics.'

Miss Vigers, then in her 50s, was devoted to her employer, Major Frank, and helped him in the garden whenever she could. She attacked stinging nettles with a special vengeance, as if offended by their disrespect. There was a sting in her own character, though, which she reserved for certain other members of staff. Mary said, 'She had a sort of antipathy for one or two people, particularly Jack Enticknap the groom, who hated her and she hated him, and we didn't exactly hate her, but we found her restricting. We used to go riding with Jack and he would always make us late for our lessons if he could, just to make her angry. And she would thump her chest and shout at him, and shout at us. But it made no difference - in the summer if it was lovely weather he used to take us to Lound to the Village Maid pub and give us ginger beer, just especially to make us late.'

When Miss Vigers left, Mary had a series of governesses, starting with an Austrian girl, who taught nothing but French and German for two years, for which Mary was ever grateful. When war broke in 1939, the young Austrian was interned. A French mademoiselle came next, but the children were being evacuated on and off to places of safety, and when Mary was at home her father soon saw the possible danger of his innocent daughter spending so much time with the soldiers who were billeted in the hall. She was finally sent away to boarding school.

The nursery rooms became vacant during the war, until another generation would come along to make fantasy charges on the rocking horse, or take imaginary pot shots out of the windows. Later the nursery

Miss Vigers doing battle with nettles

was re-established in the former kitchen on the ground floor, and the top part of the house was left to its memories. The schoolroom was eventually turned into Lord Somerleyton's office.

While the upper domestics took care of the conspicuous comforts at Somerleyton Hall, and the middle order were attending to the Crossley family's personal needs, the lower servants could be found in almost every nook and cranny, scrubbing, dusting and polishing, or tending fires and attending to every menial, manual task.

During the time of Sir Savile and Lady Phyllis Crossley, a whole colony of under-servants including maids, footmen, odd-job men and hall boys scurried about the place, busying themselves from before dawn until well after dusk. Behind the scenes they might snatch the time to joke with each other, or play tricks and flirting games, but once they were through into their employers' territory, they assumed a mantle of invisibility and hush.

They carried out their duties virtually unnoticed, as if the pristine environment was down to the work of fairies. Their appearance could be nymph-like too. Girls as young as twelve went into service, working their under-developed bodies until their very bones ached with the effort. Some seemed to miss out puberty and buxom womanhood altogether, and instead they would just seem old, always.

To the outside world their status in society was equally diminutive and maids recall that they would invent all kinds of job descriptions rather than admit to being a 'Skivvy'. Boys didn't want to marry someone who scrubbed floors for a living, they wanted someone who could cook and raise children. Their prejudice started at an early age, as local man Bertie Butcher explained. 'I went along with a servant once, I don't know if I ought to tell you that. I was about 16 or 17, I used to get a hiding for going out with a skivvy. And one night I went upstairs and chucked my coat out of the window and then I told my mother I was going outside to the toilet. And I never went to the toilet, I jumped over the wall, grabbed my coat and went down and met her. When I got home, Father was outside – was I in trouble!'

Skivvying was dirty work, and a dirty word, to boot. Even so, there was no shortage of applicants whenever the Crossleys needed new recruits. The pay and conditions may have been poor but alternatives such as factory work seemed even less attractive to most country boys and girls. In turn the Crossleys were keen to employ local people if they could, or lose the heart of their community if the young were lured away to the towns. Scrubbed up and deposited in a uniform, almost any honest, hardworking person could perform a useful task around the house, but the internal politics and strict hierarchy of the domestic regime would be a different experience altogether.

In the hall, the male servants were answerable to the butler, while the girls had the housekeeper or the cook as their boss. The lowest maids and hall boys waited on their superiors and they cleaned, tidied and tended the fires in the butler's pantry and the housekeeper's room, or Pug's Parlour as they irreverently called it. They might start as fifth housemaid and set their sights on moving up the scale, which could happen quickly when there was a rapid turnover of staff.

In general, employers had little contact with the lower domestics, so if a maid caught the eye of Phyllis, Lady Somerleyton, it was likely that something about her was out of place. She was heard to declare to her long-suffering personal maid, 'There is no class so tiresome as the servant class', to which her loyal maid nodded and agreed.

Caricature of a drunken charwoman by Lady Somerleyton's brother 'Shuggie'

Phyllis' granddaughter, Mary Birkbeck, witnessed the strict atmosphere of those days, and noticed how attitudes softened as years went by. From her experience she has concluded, 'it was more the fashion then to treat staff indifferently. Now it would be totally unacceptable.'

So servants knew better than to catch the eye. Maids would step aside and press themselves into the corridor wall as Lady Somerleyton passed by, or they would enter a room, tend to the fire and leave again without a word being exchanged. There were other times when anonymity was required. Those who were privy to dining room discussions and drawing room gossip had to join in the pretence that they had not been there at all. Footmen and parlour maids waiting at table were assumed by the diners to be deaf, and even when handing dishes they were virtually ignored.

When the author Margaret Powell began to reveal her own experience of life in service she wrote that employers saw servants as a necessary evil. At the turn of the century many articles had been written about the problem of finding good staff and ladies tut-tutted over their tea about the increasing dissatisfaction of servants with their lot. Margaret Powell said 'In the opinion of Them (the employers) we servants must never get ill, we must never dress too well and we must never have an opinion that differed from theirs.' Perhaps this seems too despotic to be true, but its veracity is borne out by example. One former servant of the Crossleys recalled Savile's anger at being presented with a doctor's bill for 2s.6d. in respect of a sick maid. He apparently railed 'I thought we only employed strong, healthy girls', and dismissed the doctor. On another occasion Phyllis berated her housekeeper for allowing a girl to wear light coloured stockings on her day off. They were only permitted to wear black. Finally, a man came close to dismissal from the Crossleys' service when it was found out that he harboured sympathies with Socialists, a group whom Sir Savile could never abide.

One new maid was lucky to get away with treating her employer with less than the usual degree of respect. Coming back to the hall one evening via the farm, she found her way blocked by a herd of bullocks, and called to an old man working nearby to shoo them away. After he had done so, she said 'Haven't you left off yet? They ought to be ashamed, making an old man like you work at this time of night!' She was horrified when the 'old man' came into the kitchen the next day and she was introduced to Lord Somerleyton. Smiling, he told the other girls that here at least was someone who had his interests at heart. In fact the incident appealed to his sense of humour to such an extent that the tale became one of his favourites at the dinner table for some time after.

For most of the staff, if they went about their business in a quiet and diligent way, their job security was assured. Without doubt though a few of them just had to be 'let go' almost as soon as they arrived. There was the housemaid who brought more than a tin trunk with her, and when her roommate saw livestock in the girl's hairbrush, she complained to the housekeeper. Others were work shy or bolshy, or, worst of all, dishonest. Then there was the problem of Human Nature.

Girls who were 'skivvies' may not have attracted genuine suitors easily, but some were like beacons of light to the moth-like male population. Having left home in their early teens they mostly knew little about 'the facts of life' except what they had seen on the farm, but the animals gave no clue that sweet talk and flirting could lead to the same thing. A pregnant girl could expect no sympathy, and if one of the dangerous home-abortion potions such as a dose of Pennyroyal pills did not work, neither would they when their condition became known. One Somerleyton girl was lucky, though. When she found herself pregnant she was told by her father, 'If it happens again, you'll be off to Oulton Workhouse'. The baby was brought up as her brother, just another mouth to feed in an already large family. In later years, the second Lady Somerleyton, Bridget, arranged a number of unofficial adoptions around the village, before such matters were properly taken on by the State.

Despite the strict regime, many servants at Somerleyton Hall did enjoy certain aspects of their lives. There were perks of all kinds, from good food to gifts from grateful visitors. The training they received was second to none, so those who wanted to leave could find new employment easily if they said they came from Somerleyton. Many of them stayed for years, and some for decades. Gertie Norton, nee Chapman, says her experience as a housemaid at the hall in the late 1920s was typical of the duties a young girl was expected to perform in exchange for her food, shelter and a small wage; in Gertie's case, that wage was five shillings a week. She still marvels at the power of endurance she had then, but she confirms that there were many good times, as she tells in her own words, 'I come to Somerleyton Hall when I was 15 and when I got there I thought, "Oh my word, what a place to come and work. I shall never stick here." I mean, young like that and on your hands and knees, I used to scrub them old passages. You used to do a certain piece each day, imagine that scrubbing with a brush and a bucket of water. That was hard, I'll tell you, didn't I have sore knees. But I did stay.'

'That first day, I come by train to Somerleyton and the chauffeur met me at the station. Ted Artis his name was, he was the second chauffeur. I met the old housekeeper Emma, she was a lovely old lady, had her little white net cap on, and long dress. We all had long dresses down to our ankles, white with pale spots on and an apron over the top, and buttoned up to the collar. I went as fifth housemaid and I finished as third. I lived in, right up at the top of the stairs, it was a small room with two beds in it and a chest of drawers and a wash stand. The window was arched, overlooking the lovely gardens and you should see the dances they had on the lawn. We used to screw ourselves, three or four of us, into the window space to look. They'd dance till half past four in the morning, and we had to get up at half past five. Emma come along and knock on everyone's door. After the morning's work you had to go to bed for two hours in the afternoon and start work again at four.'

Gertie at Somerleyton

'I never did any heavy work, the odd man did that, Smith. He was quite old, lived in the village. I did the stone floors. As well as the passage floors I done the servants hall where we all had our meals, I kept that clean, and the housekeeper's room where the lady's maid and the butler had their meals. When we all sat down in the servants' hall there was such a crowd of us. The kitchen staff never come in, it was just all the housemaids and the footmen, the chauffeurs used to come over and all. That's another thing, I had to set all the table out ready for meals.'

When Gertie was at Somerleyton, Sir Savile was elderly and less inclined to socialise, but his son and daughter-in-law, Frank and Bridget, were living at the hall and a host of young men and women frequently came to enjoy their hospitality, especially in the winter months. Gertie continues, 'We used to be scared stiff to wash the best china, 'cause when they had shooting parties we had to get all the posh china in the stillroom for their special dinners. Nobody weren't allowed to wash them, only us. Footmen weren't allowed to do it. Nothing ever got broken. All the cutlery and everything, the best of everything come out. The ballroom was beautiful when that was all set out - all lovely white chairs with pink to match the curtains. They had a lovely wooden thing with china birds on it, if there weren't one there was forty on there. We had to wash all those birds.'

Even when there was only the family at the hall, Gertie had plenty to keep her busy. As she rose from fifth housemaid to fourth and then third, her jobs changed and improved. 'Gradually I got to work upstairs and I loved it up there. The bedrooms were beautiful; the Tapestry Room, the Green Room, the Pink Room. There was one where royalty come, all the frills and lace all around the bed. I had to do all the fireplaces. I had to go into the old Lady Somerleyton's - Lady Phyllis. She'd lay in bed watching me do the fireplace, it had a big fender, you could sit on the edge of it, and that was all brass. It all had to be cleaned. She had curtains all around her bed. You didn't speak unless she spoke to you, I used to be terrified but I got used to it. I can see her now. This would be at ten, half past ten - she'd lay in bed half the day, 'cause she was old then. Downstairs she had a boudoir, that was her sitting room, that was all blue and white, beautiful.'

'Then there was him, Lord Savile, 'cause he never slept in with her, he had his own bedroom and dressing room, a lot of the bedrooms had a dressing room each. He was a lovely, rosy, round-faced man, he was a lovely old chap. But if she came along the passage, we weren't allowed to pass her, we had to stand at the side and say "Morning M'Lady". It weren't like that when Lady Bridget come. They were different altogether, very friendly. There was no standing aside when she come along, she'd laugh and talk and have a chat with you. She was beautiful.'

'I loved looking after the visitors. The ladies would come, and those that hadn't got lady's maids with them, I used to have to put the water out in the basins for them to wash, we used to have a brass watering can. And I had to unpack for them, put all their clothes away, I really enjoyed that. There was a certain way you had to hang them in the wardrobe, and their nightdresses had to be laid out properly. They never left you many tips though.'

'I stayed three years, I would have stayed longer if they gave me more money. Some girls never kept there long, they'd say the work was too hard. But the food was nice, and when the Lord and Lady went away, we went on board wages, which meant we got a bit of extra money for our food. Then we had to clean everywhere, wash everything, it took a couple of months or more. In the library, we had to take every book out and dust them and they all had to go back properly. There's hundreds. We used to love that spring-cleaning, we'd walk round the gardens, take the dogs out.' Gertie adds smiling, 'Yes, we had some good times.'

Gertie married a local bricklayer whom she met while out with Emma Jaggard, selling bagsful of dripping at 6d a pound. She moved on to work at a tuberculosis hospital where the wages were higher, but when she later went for a job at a holiday camp, the mere mention of having served at Somerleyton

Hall was reference enough for her new employer. They knew straight away that she had been thoroughly trained.

At Somerleyton, the mammoth spring cleaning programme took place at the time of what Monica Smith, nee Crossley, called The Great Annual Exodus. When Monica was a young girl in the early part of the century, her father Sir Savile held several important positions in London which meant prolonged work in the city. In addition, there was 'the Season' to occupy the thoughts and plans of the ladies. Monica explained, 'towards the end of February, we all set out for London. Our move was a tremendous undertaking, as the entire household went, except one housemaid and the odd man, who remained at Somerleyton. We had a cook, two kitchen maids, a scullery maid, butler, two footmen, valet and of course Nanny and Nurserymaid in addition to three or four housemaids.'

Out on the tiles... Jessie Redgrave on the hall roof

It was not only the family and staff who vacated the hall. Monica remembered, 'dishes, cutlery, pots and pans, and many ornaments all had to be packed into wooden cases and transported by farm lorries and by train.'

Monica used to count the days until she could get back to Somerleyton, where the silence of the countryside made her ears tingle, and where she could again hear the locals speaking in what she called 'our native tongue.'

When the family were at home, they often needed to take on extra staff to cater for the waves of guests that came, especially during the shooting season. Trusted estate workers might be brought in and decked out as footmen or butlers and girls were drafted from the village for kitchen duties. Sam Cole took this route from garden boy to hall boy, and eventually he became butler. Winifred Hardman, nee Pygall, put in several appearances in the kitchen.

She recalls, 'I was scullery maid when I was 15, then I went back twice more as second kitchen maid for the shooting seasons. Cook was Mrs Pitman, a very grand old lady. She was a Miss, but was always called Mrs. The head kitchen maid was Queenie Bartram, sister of Sam the footballer, she was in her 20's. When we were cleaning together, if I got behind she used to throw the wet floor cloth at me, so I caught up quick. As well as the kitchen maid and scullery maid there was a Mrs Folkard who used to come in daily. She went home because she was married, the rest of us lived in.'

'We started at six in the morning. Mrs Pitman always come and knocked on our door, then she went back to bed. We got up and did our work then we called her at half past seven, she was always down at eight. In the morning we wore a blue dress with a long white apron and a cap that covered most of your hair. In the afternoon, after you'd had a rest, you changed into a black dress with a little short apron. We wore black stockings and we weren't allowed to wear shoes with a rubber heel. You had to make a noise on the tiles so Mrs Pitman could hear you coming. But Mrs Pitman was not as strict as Emma Jaggard.'

Winifred was working with the family when Sir Savile died in 1935. Bridget became Lady Somerleyton, and the staff looked forward to a relaxation in the working atmosphere, but her Ladyship was no pushover, she still insisted that certain standards should be maintained. Winifred soon discovered this for herself. 'Once I won a guinea on a sweepstake and had my hair permed. When her Ladyship came down to talk with cook about menus, she was absolutely disgusted. We were supposed to have a short bob, you see.'

Winifred describes her daily workload. 'As scullery maid I looked after the boiler and blackleaded it every morning then scrubbed the scullery floor and then all the vegetables were done in there and all the washing up, all the pans and utensils. We had copper pans and the inside was done with soft soap and vinegar and the outside was done with sand, soft soap and vinegar. It was in big bowls and you grabbed it and dabbed it round. The stillroom maid did the best china in the stillroom, it was a tiny room. We did the servants' hall things in the scullery. We had big wooden sinks and we washed up in one and we rinsed in another and it was only soda in your water. And there were big wooden racks and all the plates and everything was put in them to drain.'

Contrary to many people's impression that Mrs Pitman was stern or severe, Winifred remembers the cook as being gentle and kind when it mattered. 'Every night, my hands would be red raw up to my elbows where they'd been in the deep sink. After I'd had my bath Mrs Pitman used to come with glycerine and lemon and do my hands. Then next morning it was all healed up lovely and you'd start another day.'

Winifred continues, 'Scullery maid plucked all the birds and skinned all the rabbits - 15 every week for the servants' hall pie, we used to make a big pie every week. I had to do the eyes as well as the skins, but I got 3d each for the skins. The gentry didn't have rabbit pies, we made hot meat pies for the shooting party. We had a rag and bone man used to come and gave me 3d for the skins and Mrs Pitman always used to give him some of the hot pies straight out of the oven and he used to put them in his sack with the rabbit skins. You'd see him sitting along the road having his elevenses or fourses, eating these pies. His name was Mr Markham, he lived at Oulton and they say he was a very rich man when he died.'

'When I was kitchen maid we scrubbed the kitchen floor twice a day, starting at 6 o'clock in the morning after we lit the fire. We had beautiful cream tiles you could eat off. The walls were half lavender and half cream. That bottom half was washed every day and the top half washed once a week. It was an enormous kitchen. A long fireplace with a grate that took two huge buckets of coal. The odd man filled those and pushed them under the big table, dozens of them, and each time we wanted to make up the fire two of us got one and shot it in. The range was about 20 feet long, with dampers all along that you'd pull out or push in to make it hotter or colder and we used to have to clean it all, blacklead every morning. It had four or five ovens either side and there was a thing on the end that held hot water for tea or whatever. Then up the corner we had great big pots that we put everything in so you'd always got a stock - all the bones went in it, all the vegetables, eggshells, everything.'

Winifred says that it was hot work all year round, and the steamy environment wasn't to everyone's liking. It was mostly manual work too, hard on the hands, arms, and feet, the latter having to stand all day on the cold tiled floor. She describes the scene. 'There was a long table down the middle with four places, each with a pastry board and all around that was all your utensils. Any chopping up or mixing was done there and then there was bread made every morning, and scones. The cook did all the important cooking and fancy dishes. There were no mixers or anything. Raw fish and raw meat was ground up in a pestle and mortar, kept by the icebox. We had an enormous icebox -

there was no refrigeration. This big chunk of ice used to be delivered once a week and it used to drain gradually with all the fish and meat lying round it. And the big pot underneath was always full of smelly water, we used to have to empty it daily and scour it, and swill it out with boiling water.'

Winifred agrees that there were happy times at Somerleyton, like when head kitchen maid Queenie Bartram switched on her radio in the evenings and the girls danced around the kitchen to the music of Joe Loss, Jack Payne and others. She left the Crossleys' employment in the year of Sir Savile's death, 1935. Today she still gives talks to local groups about her days at Somerleyton.

During the 1920s and 30s the butler at Somerleyton Hall was the highly respected Sam Cole. He had risen to the position by the time-honoured route, starting as a lowly hall boy and working his way up to the summit of the domestic career mountain. His apprenticeship was not all served at Somerleyton, but he spent some of his time on the staff of the Earl of Ancaster, where he learned about the intricacies of an upper domestic's work.

The Earl's family were very rich indeed, with castles in Lincolnshire and Scotland, a shooting lodge and a hall and estate in Rutland. When they moved from house to house, they had a special train to take all the staff and luggage, and even the horses, carriages and the new Rolls Royce went on board. This extravagance was far in excess of anything Sam had witnessed while working for the Crossleys, but the rituals and rules of etiquette were the same throughout the land, so the young servant kept his ears and eyes open, knowing that his skills would never be wasted.

For the shooting season the family's base was Drummond Castle and it was here that Sam learned about dining on a magnificent scale. He wrote, 'Dinner was a grand meal of six courses and took well over an hour to serve. At the end of the meal, after the savoury course had been served, the table was cleared and special plates, a half-filled bowl of water, a doily, silver knives, forks and spoons were put out for dessert. This was the time for the servants to leave the room and take up a position outside the door. After about 10 minutes the door would open and the ladies would withdraw to the drawing room for coffee and liqueurs. The men were then free to use strong language and tell any kind of stories they liked, and believe me, some of the stories they told were very spicy indeed.'

Sam knew better than to repeat any of the 'spicy stories', and his tact and integrity stood him in good stead. However, one incident did bring a blush to his cheeks. He had been promoted to the position of third footman, bringing him in closer contact with his employers and their guests - a little too close, in fact. 'I shall never forget my first day waiting at table. I had been told to be very careful when handing dishes to ladies, especially those wearing very low-cut gowns. I must not stand too close to them, but if on the other hand I stood too far away, they would be forced to lean over with disastrous results. I did not fully understand what this meant, but I was soon to learn.'

'While serving one lady who was wearing a dangerously low-cut dress, I did not stand close enough to her. She leaned out to reach the dish and to my great alarm, out popped a certain part of her anatomy. I stood gazing in horror and fascination. Then, with a quick jerk and a few wriggles, all was replaced. Somehow I managed to continue to serve and was very worried as I felt I would be blamed. However, nothing was said and it was a lesson to me how not to wait at table.'

At 6'3 in height, Sam cut a dignified figure in his black uniform suit, and in other forms of attire, too. His duties while in London included hall duty - opening the door to visitors. For this he had to wear breeches, silk stockings and a smart red, green and gold-braided tailcoat. It was a typical uniform for hall staff, very fashionable for the time, but most uncomfortable for the wearer. Sam recalled, 'I was very glad when one day, just before the end of the Season, we were told that in future we need not powder our hair. Apparently the practice had gone out of fashion. This was a great relief as we used to use violet powder and flour, which made our scalps itch, and scratching was definitely not permitted.'

Now Sam was promoted again, this time to second footman. It was not only his job title that was to change. 'I had to answer to the name of George. Samuel was not considered a suitable name for a footman and as the man I replaced was called George, that was to be my name. Probably his name was not George either!' This practice of naming a servant according to their job was a convenience many employers used to save themselves the bother of learning the names of their employees. It was not common at Somerleyton but nicknames were widely used and one footman, William Beechener, or Willikins to the children, was a firm favourite.

Mary Birkbeck said 'William was the first footman to whom we were devoted and I vividly remember him teaching me to swim in the lake. He was known as Willikins and when I was a little older and allowed to go down to lunch on Sundays in my frilly dress, I would go through the dining room and he'd still be laying the table and I'd say to him, "What are we having for lunch today, Willikins?" and he'd say "It's going to be a fancy lunch today, Miss Mary, you're going to walk round the table and fancy you've had it."

Of course, the footmen wore lovely blue livery, they had buff coloured waistcoats with brass buttons and blue cut-away coats with silver buttons. When the parents were away the footmen would jump over the garden wall onto the terrace to make their coat tails fly to amuse us.'

William eventually left the Crossleys to become a butler at Barton Hall in Norfolk, and married his sweetheart Violette, the Somerleyton nurserymaid. In 1948, on the day Violette gave birth to their second daughter, they received a letter from Lady Bridget asking if William would consider coming back to Somerleyton as butler. 'You remember Cole's house in the Street; that would be yours', offered her Ladyship. But the Beecheners had had another letter, from Sam Cole himself, commenting about the present incumbent, 'the butler is a discharged soldier, suffering with varicose veins. I should not think being there would be a rest cure for him'. Nevertheless they were tempted, remembering their happy days at the hall.

William in the Somerleyton football team, 1935

Finally William wrote to Lady Somerleyton and thanked her kindly, but said they were settled and would prefer not to move. Loyal and devoted servants like the Beecheners were becoming increasingly hard to find in an age when it was easier to move from place to place, and the working class man and woman would not take orders without question. As society became more relaxed and permissive, staff at the hall became more reserved, and succeeding generations of Somerleyton children are unlikely to find servants who will jump to amuse them. Even so, the dignity and affection of those footmen and maids will always bring a smile to the lips of Mary Birkbeck and her brothers.

William Beechener with Nick at Fritton Lake

Reference for William Beechener. It reads; *'Dear Lord Somerleyton, I have every confidence in recommending William Beechener, he is a really good hard working man, and I think he has intelligence and is honest, sober and willing. He comes of a good family in our village, most honest and hard working. I do not want to say too much in case you are disappointed in him, but I can thoroughly recommend him as the right type of servant, and if you take him I am sure he will serve you well.'*

Chapter 6

Taking Care of Business and Pleasure

———————————— ෙ ෙ ————————————

ong before paying guests were allowed in to see the stately interior of
Somerleyton Hall, people were coming by road, rail and even river to
marvel at the immaculate and colourful gardens. On open days, visitors could
view the neat lawns where lords and ladies danced, and wander through
pathways where annuals formed great swathes of colour, or where perennials
stood tall like guards of honour. They would be drawn on through pergolas
over which roses, clematis and wisteria scrambled to peep down at the intruders,
and finally the braver daytrippers might risk missing their lift home by taking
up the challenge to get lost in the maze.

For more than a century, articles written about the Somerleyton gardens
have poured praise on the designer glasshouses, the fine statuary and the ornate
clocktower with its historic connection to London's Big Ben, but it is the
sound of the striking bell that has the power to cause the occasional visitor to
stop in their tracks. They pause and move on, remembering how their day of
toil would begin as the 6.30 chime rang out. They are former gardeners of
Somerleyton.

In the 1940s a young girl named Nancy James was on the staff, gardening
from dawn until dusk for wages of £2 a week. It was heavy, dirty work, although
not impossible for a fit country girl and Nancy didn't mind the digging, weeding,
and pruning. However, there was one job that she dreaded, and just the thought
of it still makes her wince. She explains, 'I used to clip that maze with hand

clippers - it took weeks and weeks and weeks. I think every foot of it is printed on my mind still.'

Nancy continues, 'It was a very square hedge, in winter it used to collect the snow and my colleague Dolly Smith and I used to sweep the snow off the top with a birch broom and then find where it wanted clipping. We'd work our way through to the centre. There in the middle is a lovely place; there's a little garden and a thing where you can sit down. But we were glad to keep going, to keep warm in wintertime. We hated when we knew the maze was coming up to be clipped. I don't know how many miles of hedge that is.'

Nancy was a stockily built girl, brought up on a farm in Lound where her father was horseman and her grandfather Joe Crack ran the village store. The farm was rented from Lord Somerleyton and as a teenager Nancy had delivered milk to the hall on her specially adapted bicycle, but it had never occurred to her that one day she would be weeding those acres of flowerbeds that she passed on the way. She explains 'I went to work up there because of the war time, you see. You had to do something in the way of war work and you either had to work on the land or go into ammunitions. But country people don't like going away, do they? Not real country people. Course, at that time they took all the men in the army, that's why they had to have female workers.'

Even for a stout farmer's daughter, weeding was a back breaking routine. 'We were always on the herbaceous borders and flower beds and the pergola. They had these huge great beds of separate flowers - a whole great big bed of delphiniums and they had a beautiful one of lupins, ever so long. We used to have to stake all these lupins in case the wind blew them over.'

Mud was an occupational hazard, and yet Nancy's uniform consisted of a white shirt, white jumper, black trousers and blue blazer, all of which she had to buy for herself. She recalls there being ten gardeners at the time, and their brief breaks from the elements were spent in a shed they called the Mess Room. 'It had a big round 'Tortoise' stove for warmth. Some of them used to put a metal cup or something on top to warm tea out of a bottle - they used to have it in a bottle in those days, not a flask. We'd have our 'nineses' in there and our lunch.'

The mess room gave the gardeners a chance to chat and get to know each other, says Nancy. 'I met my husband there, he couldn't go in the war because he was practically blind in one eye, so he went into horticulture. He lived in the bothy with a boy by the name of Enticknap and a woman used to come up from the village to make the beds and cook their dinner each day. Harry was ever so unhappy at the bothy. There were four rooms but they were very bare, you just had a bed and a dressing table. In the living room there was just hard chairs to sit on and a table. I think they all used to spend their evenings down at the pub.'

Harry Pudney was in charge of the fruit houses, where peaches, plums and figs were grown. Nancy admits she did fall victim to temptation if a ripe fig dropped on the floor, even though eating the fruit was strictly forbidden. The tasty supplement to rationed food was like manna from Heaven. 'You weren't supposed to eat them', she adds, 'but I used to walk through the fruit houses and if there was one on the floor I'd pick it up. They were beautiful.'

Nancy and Harry married in 1942 and left Somerleyton Hall two years later, after a disagreement with the head gardener, who at the time was Tom Smith. He was a hard taskmaster, but, remembers another former gardener, he knew how to keep his workforce under tight control and, says Clifford Dann, he often had to teach his juniors from scratch. 'I'd only done farm work before I went there in about 1935,' says Clifford. 'I went there at 17 - Lord Somerleyton's aunt arranged the interview. I got a job in the greenhouses. That was living in the bothy, you buy your own food, you get a wage but half of it went on food, you see. I started at about 15s. a week.'

Clifford soon found out there was more to his job than daytime pruning and watering, at times he was on duty round-the-clock. 'Every third week you had to stop up there all the time, you weren't allowed outside the gardens. And at ten o'clock at night you would have to go and make sure of what the temperature was outside and you'd log that and then you would have to take that again at seven o'clock the next morning, so they would know whether you were there or not. That was a way of keeping you in. Through the winter months you had the fires to stoke up for the greenhouse heating, course that was all coal fires. Fresh flowers were grown all year round and the hall would have fresh flowers three times a week. Like carnations, and lilies. And there was fruit - peaches, grapes and figs.'

Those forbidden delicacies had also proved just too much for Bertie Butcher, an earlier gardener, to resist. Bertie worked under the formidable head gardener, Fred Hanson. Some descibe Mr Hanson as a 'gentleman gardener'; very formal and diligent, he was 'Sir' to all his men. The fear of Mr Hanson's disapproval could not outweigh the sight and smell of a luscious pear, however, as Bertie recalled with relish. 'There were some lovely pears, they were trained on the walls, and one day I thought, "Blast, I'm going to have one", and I reached up. "Leave that alone, boy!" old Hanson shouted. Then one day he sent me over, 'cause we used to have to get fruit for the Hall, we had to go and gather some raspberries. Cor, we had a lovely armful of raspberries. He say "You're helping yourself, boy, ain't you?" I say "Yes". He give me another job after that, he wouldn't let me go back no more. But there was a pit where we used to have to cart all the grass, and I'd go and collar a nectarine and go down the pit and eat it. You couldn't buy that sort of fruit.'

Lord Somerleyton confirms that the precious produce was guarded fiercely. 'I remember Mr Smith the head gardener who left us just after the second war; if we took any fruit he always noticed, if we took one fig or one grape off a bunch he always noticed straight away. I remember getting into an awful row for taking some peaches or figs out of those greenhouses and not telling anyone, and of course he knew immediately because he'd watch them 24 hours a day'.

Head gardener Tom Smith standing proudly beneath the pergola

In wet weather, Bertie Butcher and his colleagues had to scrub out those glasshouses, washing the glass and cleaning the mildew from the woodwork. His training in gardening had started early. Bertie said, 'They couldn't learn me nothing at school – I only counted up to three. So old Billy Grieg the schoolmaster used to send me out into his garden and he give me a jam jar and I used to have to pick caterpillars off his greens.'

Bertie and his schoolmates did look forward to their annual visit to Somerleyton gardens on Valentine's day when they gathered together in the enormous winter garden.

A great leaded glass conservatory covering more than 100 square feet, the winter garden had been built for Sir Samuel Morton Peto as part of the rebuilding works at the hall, and its design owed much to London's Crystal Palace. Its centrepiece, a sultry, illuminated glass dome, housed a marble fountain which was described in the Garden Magazine of 1872 as being 'supported on rock-work by four dolphins and surmounted by a marble statue of the Nymph of the Lily from the top of which the water is thrown through a jet to a height of nearly 50 feet. Water is also emitted from a number of small jets and from the mouths of dolphins situated near the base of the rockwork. This fountain is surrounded by a basin some 50 feet in diameter.'

On either side of the entrance to the winter garden, great gilded cages with stained glass inserts housed finches and canaries, whose trilling songs serenaded those who strolled among the lush, tumbling greenery.

The Somerleyton Winter Garden

There were fine statues alongside the walkways and great urns added an eastern touch. Unfortunately, one of these was broken during the annual Valentine's Day treat for children of the estate and they were kept out after that. The children didn't mind at all, their favourite part of the ritual was receiving a penny and a bun, and being sent off to lose themselves in the maze.

Geoffrey Howes, who was a contemporary of Bertie's, wrote

about his childhood memory of the event in a booklet entitled Valentine Quartet. He said, 'A grinning gardener, stout and very obviously clad in Sunday best, rattles open the doors. "Go on," he says, "through yer trot – and don't make market pigs of yerselfs!"' Once through the gates, the children stare around them at the velvet lawns and mighty specimen trees. Geoffrey continues, 'Here and there pose statues without even a warm smile on. A moment, then the awe of one bright youth is abruptly forgotten. "Look! Look! You can see her ***" To everyone's deep regret the headmaster cuts him short.'

He tells how the children are ushered into the smaller conservatory where, 'A long-faced footman in green livery is opening arched double doors ...beyond him, a floor of intricate mosaic is edged by twisting and spraying shrubs and more Grecian statues. Again young eyes linger upon bodily bounties, but this time no-one says a word. The sense of awe is now almost absolute.'

The spell is broken when the children see the piles of bright new pennies and freshly baked buns that were to be handed out by Lord and Lady Somerleyton. 'They wait, some shuffling feet on gratings from which cokey air wafts warmly, some whispering "It's them!" The grey-suited Lord sporting a cropped moustache and with one hand characteristically in pocket, his elegantly green-suited lady smiling at his side.' After the distribution of the goodies, during which Savile remembers every child's name, the crowd would spill out onto the lawn where their host delivered a short speech about the tradition of the Valentine's Day treat, before signalling that the children could run and play. Geoffrey continues, 'The youngsters, suddenly freed of all restraints, feverishly munching their buns (except for the odd pieces knotted into handkerchiefs for extra-special mums), fling arms high and speed in all directions Eventually of course, every child pelts towards the maze.' The race is on to reach the middle first, and Geoffrey describes the laughter and frustration as smart-alec boys find their memories have let them down, and little girls threaten to tell parents about the obscenities that are heard through the prickly walls as each blind alley is found.

True to his word, the headmaster leaves lost children behind in the labyrinth until they all emerge and try to sneak away without being spotted. Geoffrey concludes, 'you must pass through what is once more Forbidden Territory at a time when his Lordship might well be prowling vigilantly around.'

Savile was indeed possessive about his privacy, and when he retreated back into the winter garden, he could shut the doors and imagine himself to be in a faraway land, among tropical ferns and damp creepers draped with scented blooms. The winter garden was a masterpiece of Victorian opulence. It provided a perfect microclimate even in the depths of winter and its beauty and ingenuity were said to be 'unsurpassed by anything of its kind in Europe'. Adjacent to it was a palm house supplying stately plants for the house, and the corridor between the two conservatories housed award-winning Japanese chrysanthemums, grown by head gardener Fred Hanson.

The whole structure was a world of its own, but it was an expensive luxury whose days were numbered. It needed two men to work there full-time, stoking the boilers, watering the plants and tending the thousands of pot plants that brought year-round colour to the hall. It used over 1700 yards of piping, it consumed tons of coke in its two boilers, and copious amounts of gas for the lighting. The glorious winter garden fell victim to Savile's economy drive in 1914. He tried offering it to local authorities for public use, but there were no takers and so the enormous task of dismantling this giant's greenhouse

Demolition of the winter garden

Sir Savile's daughter Monica commented that her father had 'always intended' to pull down the winter garden - perhaps it was just a little too extravagant for his taste, but the coming of the Great War and the need to make savings seems to have been the catalyst for his action.

Monica often talked about the happy times she had around the hall gardens, making friends with the characters working there. Her lonely pre-war childhood was enriched by those friendships and she remembered them all her life. She recorded some of their jobs too, giving an insight to their widely varied duties, for which the twenty or so men were paid an average £1 10s. a fortnight, or £39 a year.

Monica said 'Frederick Hanson was head gardener for over 35 years, a wonderful gardener. He was very strict with his men but gave them a first rate training. There was Billy Crawford who worked on the lawns; he had a bad stutter, closing his eyes and throwing his head back, to help the words out. He suffered much with his feet. He said he washed them once in Condis Fluid, but that made them worse, so he said, "I aren't gonna wash 'em no more!" Charlie Betts worked in the kitchen garden and used to bring the vegetables up to the kitchen every morning, pulling them along on an open truck. He was always a bit lame, I don't know why. And I'm never sure whether he was Charlie or Billy, for we always called him Betts.'

'Also I used to spend hours with Jimmy Orford. I see him him now, finishing a beautiful job and wetting his scythe before going on to the next place, and singing a little ditty; "Said the right foot to the left foot and the left foot to the right foot, January, February... March!" and off he went. My father used to open the garden to the public every Thursday in summer and Jimmy used to take the appropriate notices round in a barrow and then walk down the front drive and sit at the main gate, wearing a special dark blue coat and cap.'

'A great many people used to drive out in charabancs from Lowestoft and other places, and his duty was to count them all and pass up the tickets. Not more than four persons per horse was allowed. If there were more, they had to get out and walk the mile to the garden door. It would be a considerable walk in addition to the tour of the garden, including the ever popular maze, which added 400 yards if you got to the centre without a mistake. There were notice boards asking visitors not to walk on the grass or pick the flowers. At 5pm the gardens closed and all was returned to normal. The entrance money went to local charities.'

Monica added that the Somerleyton lawns were a source of great pride and special care was taken of them. She said 'the grass was all cut by a pony, guided by a man with a rope rein - he had to guide the big mowing machine and empty the grass from the grass box into a large barrow at intervals. Our pony always wore leather mowing shoes on the lawns, to prevent marking the turf with its sharp horseshoes.'

In the second war, the gardens suffered a great deal from the necessity to supply as much fruit and vegetables as possible, and from the incursion of evacuees, soldiers and temporary staff. Eventually the flower beds and lawns would recover, and nowadays, apart from the increasing use of machinery to take over the lengthy jobs of mowing, clipping and rubbish disposal, the garden at Somerleyton Hall remains largely in the same format today as it was a century ago.

The winter garden was replaced by a loggia, later covered over to provide a large garden room, and an impressive parterre - a great white mosaic - was taken up during the second war in case its luminous effect at night attracted enemy bombers.

The parterre, 1936

The 300 foot long pergola is still resplendent with climbers, the restored glasshouses glisten with fruit in season and visitors can walk among the great colonies of Sir Savile's beloved rhododendrons. No visit is complete without a wander through the maze, where pride must be left outside or it will be lost in a dead-end. The aged yews have crowded together for more than 150 years and their secret is shared only by the Somerleyton family and their team of faithful gardeners, past and present.

Outside the hall, the Lords and Ladies of Somerleyton rarely had contact with staff except when it came to their favourite sporting pastimes. Then, when they wanted to shoot game or hop into the saddle of a flighty hunter, their safety and enjoyment was dependent on their gamekeepers and grooms.

Shooting parties were major events which lasted up to ten days, with guests and their entourage moving into the hall for the duration. There would be evenings of dining and dancing, followed by a whole day's sport, when rabbit, duck, partridge and pheasant were all fair game. As always there were codes of etiquette, and the less important guests knew the value of passing tips to keepers, so that they might be given a good position on the field.

A great draw for any sportsman was the estate's king-sized duck pond, Fritton Decoy, which was home to thousands of water fowl. The lake, reputedly dug out in the 12th century at the same time as the Norfolk broads, is a two mile stretch of spring-fresh water, with fingers cut into the peat and wire-netted tunnels for gloves; these were special traps for catching whole flocks of birds at a time.

Fritton Lake

Kathleen Rix, niece of the agent Kerry, described the procedure for killing ducks in 1887. 'One Sunday we were taken to see the ducks decoyed at Fritton, and afterwards we wished we hadn't gone. The head keeper met us and took us down to the lake, where there were some rush screens along the bank and a net spread across the corner of the water. Some other keepers were there and also a retriever which was trained to keep trotting round and round the screens to attract the ducks.'

'We were told not to make a noise and everyone hid behind the screens while the dog went round and round. Presently the ducks began to swim up the lake to see what the dog was doing, and when they were close enough the keepers jumped out from behind the screens with a shout. The frightened ducks flew into the corner underneath the net and then the net was drawn. After that we turned away our heads, for it was horrible watching the poor things having their necks wrung.'

Sometimes as many as a thousand birds could be killed in a session in this way, so the meat would be free from lead shot. Kathleen added that Prince Edward was taken to see the operation during one of his visits and, she said, 'He wanted to see what was going on, so he stood up to look and Mr Page, the head keeper, who didn't know who he was, came behind him and took him by the shoulders and said "Get down, Sir!" The Prince of Wales couldn't have been offended, because he gave Mr Page a sovereign when he went away.'

Whether or not the keeper had recognised his monarch, Harry Page was fortunate to have got away with the faux-pas. Had he received his marching orders, few of the village ladies would have been sorry to see him go; along with the usual trophies of dead vermin that keepers traditionally hung on their 'gibbet' to demonstrate their efficiency, it was said that cats' tails were often among his gruesome bunting. He vowed to have a waistcoat made out of cats' skins, and suspiciously soft and colourful rugs were rumoured to adorn his home. Cats were public enemy number one in the eyes of a keeper, and anyone who kept them as pets had to keep them away from his game birds, or face the consequences.

Gamekeeper at Fritton decoy

Generally, the Somerleyton gamekeepers didn't mind being labelled eccentric or unsavoury. It helped to deter small boys and would-be poachers from helping themselves to the rabbits and birds which were strictly reserved for the guns of the baronet and his guests. However, one keeper came under suspicion when he asked friends to help chase pheasants onto his 'patch' before a shoot, so nobody would realise that the population was much smaller than might be expected. The shortfall was eventually noticed.

In the 1920s the head keeper was Paddy Welling, another formidable character, who meted out his own forms of punishment for anyone caught out of place on his territory. A poem by local marshman and entertainer, Tommy Crawford, tells the tale of one such incident when three youths were co-opted by Welling to help as beaters at a shoot. The weather put paid to the day's sport, so, continued Tommy,

'Orders came from up the top, "Dismiss the men there please",
And each was given beer or pop, his venison and cheese.
So all went home their various ways but the three, I'm sad to tell,
Decided on another route, Peg Gates via Wicker Well.
Now this was strictly private, but it mattered not because
They'd the freedom of the borough, for they knew where Paddy was.'

The poem goes on to say how the three lads borrowed a punt and took it out on the lake, resulting in one of them falling into the water. Tommy added,

'They quickly hauled him in the boat and planned to make for shore,
But ere their minds could be made up there came a mighty roar,
Which echoed loud throughout the woods like thunder to the three
They looked at once towards the shore - four keepers by the tree!
"Bring in that boat" roared Paddy, "and make it pretty sharp
And by the time I've done with you, you'll wish you had a harp".
They tried to land the other side, twas much too boggy there,
So Nelson, Drake and Raleigh turned round in dire despair.
Till once again the shore was reached and as they touched the hard
The sticks came down from left and right while they were off their guard
Each scrambled to his feet somehow and scarpered to the lane
To face the journey home once more by the route by which they came.
A bedraggled looking trio, an awe inspiring lot!'

Paddy wanted chaps for beating and, sure, that's what he got!

During the 1960s Frank Cullum was a keeper on the estate, working first under Fred Ollett the head keeper. Frank wrote a book about his keepering days, entitled Both Sides of the Fence, in which he said that he and his wife 'both realised this was an area of great natural beauty. We visited the hall and viewed the gardens and as my duties took me all over the estate, I was very impressed.'

By this time there were only two decoys or 'pipes' in operation on Fritton Lake. Frank continues 'I ran the decoy for four seasons until His Lordship decided to call it a day and close it down. We would only shoot the lake during the season at appropriate times. This decision had disastrous results when it came to my livelihood. I was paid a bonus on the amount of duck that I caught and the feathers were a handy perk. Some of the feathers on the shoulders and flanks of the mallard drakes are used for making fishing flies. I collected all the feathers that were of use and sent them to the fur and feather merchants who paid up to one pound for an ounce of them.' Frank said that one reason for the closure of the pipes was that public reaction had turned against the indiscriminate killing of wildfowl on such a large scale.

There was still plenty of work to do with rearing pheasants and attending the shoots, and Frank describes the good-natured banter and occasional tricks played between the keepers, who were especially competitive on shooting days. He says he came unstuck one day when head keeper Fred Ollett sent him to fetch a fallen bird; 'Ollett said "There's a bird down over there", pointing in the direction of the gardens. I took a dog and went off and unknowingly entered the famous maze. From then on, after finding the bird, I seemed to spend a considerable amount of time trying to get out, until Ollett came to rescue me!'

Fred Ollett died in 1961 and the obituary in the parish newsletter was one that any keeper might have wished for. As well as praising his great knowledge and pride in his work it added 'Wednesday was the end of the shooting season. Fittingly enough, a few hours after the last shot had been fired Ollett was laid to rest in the peace of Somerleyton churchyard, only a stone's throw from one of his best woods. He worked for three generations of the Crossley family and with them, his fellow countrymen and his family, led a full and happy life...Fred Ollett had a good season.'

The Somerleyton estate is surrounded by water and Frank Cullum adds that this meant his game birds were seldom troubled by foxes. Even so, hunting was another much-loved pastime at Somerleyton, and successive Lords Somerleyton have been master of their local hunt. They have shared a love of horse racing too – the second baron was a fine jockey himself - and they have tried just about every mounted sport from polo to point-to point.

Years ago, the horses in the stables were treated with almost as much care as their owners. One of the best-remembered grooms, John 'Jack' Enticknap, had been a friend of Frank Crossley since their soldiering days together in the first war, and Jack's letters to his master had helped Frank through the harrowing times as a prisoner. Eventually Jack resumed his job as groom in peacetime and in 1929 he moved with Frank and his young family to Somerleyton Hall. Jack was put in charge of all the satin-coated steeds, and he could not have wished for more. He had been wounded in the Great War, it left him with a disability in one elbow but he remained a first-class horseman all his life. His son Ken confirms, 'All he thought about was his horses. When he was laid in his bed in his last few hours, he was still talking about his horses.'

Jack Enticknap

Mary and Bill learning to ride

Jack taught all the Somerleyton children to ride, and they loved him dearly. He had his own large family - a wife and six sons, one of whom was named after his employer and friend, Francis Savile Crossley. He was demanding as a father, but even more so with the lads in the stables. Ken was one of them, and there is wry humour in his twinkling blue eyes as he recalls the daily routine. 'Yes, Father was very strict in the stables. In the morning we used to start about half past five and be out exercising the horses at half past six. Every morning, snow or rain, 'til half past eight.'

After his own breakfast, Ken would be back to groom the horses and clean their stables. In the afternoon he had more jobs. 'We'd clean the tack, clean the windows, scrub more stables out, even polish the brass door knobs in the stable yard.' Ken would have another meal break and return to make the horses comfortable for the night, finishing at around 7 o'clock.

Ken was so afraid of his father that he didn't dare ask for time off – he would ask his mother to make the request for him. Mostly he worked up to 70 hours a week for which he was paid 9s. in the 1930s. It was by no means easy money. He continues, 'Sometimes I could have cried with the cold when we were out riding. One day I couldn't hold my horse; that touched the horse in front and that kicked out and it caught me in the shin. The old doctor looked at the cut and he said, "look, there's your bone". He put a bandage on it and I went back to work. I've still got the scar.' Another time, says Ken, 'I had some of my teeth knocked out by a horse I was feeding. Those horses were highly strung, we used to feed them up and you had to be on your toes with them. You'd get kicks and knocks, but that was all part of the job. Once a post van frightened the horse I was riding and it bolted - that swung round into a farmyard and threw me over the wall into the muck heap.'

When he and the horses were cleaned up, Ken had reason to be proud of his handiwork. 'Course the horses did look smart, they were all clipped out and had the rugs on with 'F.C.' on the corners, for Frank Crossley. Before we went out exercising we used to oil their hooves so they used to shine, and we'd take six out at a time, that looked nice.'

Sometimes he rode out alone, and at least once he regretted it. 'I went out the front drive instead of going the usual route. Well, I was about three or four mile away from here and a pheasant flew up. The horse shied, well I was ready for that, but then that reared and off I came. I started to walk back, but they found the horse looking over the stable door and 'course they all went looking for me. But I was walking home a different way. When I got back Lord Somerleyton said, "You should tell people where you're going. Now *you* go and look for *them*." He didn't very often get angry with me but he did that morning.'

After the second war, Frank, now Lord Somerleyton, began breeding horses and Ken's job involved breaking in the youngsters. He adds, 'I thought it was a bit dangerous, and sometimes I used to be thrown off, so I asked for a pay rise and I got 6d a week, backdated two months.'

Ken's father Jack retired in 1960 and he lived on the estate until his death ten years later at the age of 80. Ken continued at the stables until 1963 when he became seriously ill. After a break working in Lowestoft, he returned to work on the estate until he retired. Even though Ken hasn't ridden for more than 30 years, local people still know where to come if they want to learn a thing or two about the secrets of horse management.

For successive owners of Somerleyton hall to have any chance of spare time for leisure, they needed to delegate large areas of responsibility to trusty employees. With an estate which at one time amounted to over 6,000 acres of farmland, woods, and parkland, it was essential to have help with the management and the books. At an early stage, Sir Savile Crossley looked around for someone special to act as his 'right-hand man'.

The estate agent's job required a good head for figurework, an all-round knowledge of farming practice, and an aptitude for dealing with people, whether they were VIP visitors or the most cantankerous of tenants and labourers. With such a large area to cover, the agent had to be the sort to motivate men without always looking over their shoulder, and to cultivate a network of reliable workers who would act as his eyes and ears when he was not there in person. A local lad in his early twenties might not seem the obvious choice for such a responsible position, but Kerry Rix got the job and held onto it for more than 40 years.

George Kerry Rix was the son of the Somerleyton schoolmaster, and he was always known by his mother's maiden name of Kerry. His parents had lost six children at an early age so their two remaining sons were all the more precious to them. Kerry, like his father, was a short man with a great bristling moustache and whiskers. His hair went grey at an early age, and his big bushy eyebrows overshadowed his keenly observant eyes. Some people loved him, some despised him, but most respected him.

Kerry Rix

For Kerry, a job on the Somerleyton estate was close to ideal; there he found a good wage, a pleasant tied cottage near to his parents and in Somerleyton Hall he found himself a wife. The last agent to be directly employed on the estate, Tom Flatt, described the job. 'A traditional country estate had numerous heads of department, so there'd be a head gardener, head gamekeeper, repairman, forester etc. The agent would be responsible for all those departments and there was an estate clerk who did the books and paid out the wages and so on. Then there'd be the farm tenants and the house tenants all requiring attention, perhaps needing repairs done. They all paid rent of course. The farm tenants paid their rent twice a year, what was known as a rent audit, and they were given entertainment to induce them to turn up.' The estate office was at Kerry's house, so he was never really free from his work.

The estate accounts of 1875 show Kerry's wage of £100 a year divided between five accounts to reflect how his time was spent managing the hall, woods, garden, and game departments and attending to his employers' private business. There were many other headings too, including the stables and the hunt kennels, the church and the school, for which Sir Savile was responsible in those days.

Kerry kept fortnightly accounts of the work and wages of all the estate men; typical entries show the time worked by 24 woodsmen on jobs such as planting and cutting rhododendrons, cutting and faggotting wood and making fencing. There were 20 men at work in the gardens and the engineers were tracked too, five of them were busy flushing drains, or repairing a turnip cutter. Four painters were in the school house and in the hall, six joiners were repairing the hen coops and the pigeon house, sharpening and using steam saws, and making gates, while seven bricklayers had tasks in the hall which included sweeping the chimneys.

Some of these were the same people doing different jobs on different days, as their job title was more a convenience than recognition of a profession. One day the woodsmen would be chopping trees and another they could be called up to the hall to beat carpets. Their wages varied greatly too. In 1909 a junior was receiving just 10d a day and a senior engineer taking home 5s.

Income from the estate cottage rents was listed in detail - there were more than 60 of them at an average rent of £5 a year. Then there were allotments for which the villagers paid half yearly, mostly at 6s. a rood which was a quarter of an acre, or 3s. for half that size, 20 perches.

Kerry Rix was much more than just a pen-pusher, he spent a lot of time touring the estate by pony and trap, dealing with tenants and estate workers face to face. Out of hours he did much for charity, and sat with the board of the Mutford and Lothingland Guardians, who had responsibility for the local workhouse and the distribution of Parish Relief to the poor.

Kerry and his wife had no children of their own but he was a great favourite with his young relatives. When his nieces came to stay in Somerleyton in 1887 Kathleen wrote in her diary, 'Uncle Kerry is always teasing us, chiefly about the Band of Hope…Uncle says we have broken our pledge because there was sherry in the trifle we had for dinner.' She described the relationship between her aunt and uncle as warm and full of humour. 'Aunt Elizabeth is very fond of Uncle,' she wrote, 'you can tell it by the way she smiles at him and pats his hand.'

Kerry Rix was an independent man, not the sort to follow the flock. Kathleen said, 'When we are staying at Laurel Cottage we do not have to go to Chapel on Sunday. We go for long walks with Uncle instead, all over the estate, where other people do not go. It gives me such a nice feeling when we go through a gate marked Strictly Private'. No doubt Kerry would have been casting a critical eye over the state of the woods and fencing, or watching out for any signs of poaching.

He enjoyed many privileges and it would have been easy to abuse his position by lining his own pockets, but Kerry had to be above temptation. He was entrusted with large sums of money and he was responsible for Savile's negotiations when buying property or even when defending his land. Kerry spent two years compiling masses of evidence to support a claim against the Lowestoft Water and Gas Company about 42 acres of land around the Decoy which was affected by their new water scheme. The Lowestoft Journal reported the hearing in December 1900; 'Mr George Kerry Rix, F.S.I., agent to Sir Savile Crossley, was the first witness examined. He furnished the Umpire with full particulars of the several pieces of land, which had been taken by the company for the purposes of establishing and protecting a water supply, and explained the damage which in his opinion would result. Witness had formed an estimate of the value, which he put at £4,557.'

The claim was pushed up over £6,000 by including loss of rents, sporting rights and timber, but after counter-arguments from the Water Company's barrister and various surveyors' opinions, the final settlement was just over £4,000. By this time Sir Savile had a new adversary; he was in South Africa taking on the Boers, leaving Lady Crossley in charge.

Next, Kerry became a manager of the local school and as another sideline he acted as agent for the Norwich Union Fire Insurance Society - Somerleyton Estate was one of his clients. No matter how many other schemes Kerry became involved with, his diligence in his estate duties never wavered. Every acre of land and everything on it was protected for his employer by fair means and even, some might say, foul.

In one instance a farm tenant came unstuck when Kerry and his men used a devious trick to prove the farmer's dog was being used for poaching. The farmer's son, Billy Richmond, tells the tale; 'A funny thing Father told me, he said "When I was young and first had dealings with Kerry Rix he tried so many things on me, thinking I was vulnerable, in the transactions we had, I had a tremendous desire to give his old whiskers a good tug."'

Billy goes on, 'When he was courting my mother he used to walk her home at night and he'd have his big dog with him. Well the keepers were determined to catch him and have this dog put down 'cause they didn't like him running the rabbits. So they used to wait for him over the wall at the top of Church Hill and as the dog used to come walking back, he'd peep through the gate to see if there was a rabbit out on the park. Well, they would release a rabbit and 'course the dog would be after it and catch the rabbit and bring it back to his master and they'd have him. Then he'd have to go up and see Kerry Rix who'd say he had to have this dog put down. He used to wind the old man up terribly, he said he couldn't have the dog put down because it wasn't his dog - in fact it was his father's dog. They had it shot in the end, though.'

The Richmonds at work on their landholding near the brickfields

Kerry took his work very seriously but he did have sympathy for the farmers when they went through hard times, like during the floods of 1912. That event is also described by Billy Richmond, whose father was renting land from the Somerleyton estate. 'That night came the storm of 1912 when all this area through here, through the Waveney Valley was flooded. All the ears on the barley were stripped off by hailstones in the thunder storm, so he lost the crop.' Billy's father was not deterred though, and like his fellow farmers he came through the lean times as best he could and took every opportunity to get on when the conditions were in his favour.

During the First World War Kerry presided over tribunals in Lowestoft, hearing the cases of men who claimed they should be exempt from call-up. Farming was one of the reasons for exclusion from duty, and Kerry was the first to understand how a livelihood and a whole community could suffer when all the fittest men were away.

After the war, Savile, now Lord Somerleyton, insisted that ex-servicemen should be given priority whenever land came up for rent, and as a result Jack Prettyman, survivor of the horrors of Passchendaele, was granted the tenancy of Mill Farm. He heard about the chance in typical local fashion, according to his son David. 'He had met my mother, then called Trixie Chapman, and they were planning to marry. One day grandfather Chapman came jogging along in his pony and cart and he said, "Do you want a farm, Boy?" Father said he did, "Well, Mill Farm is coming up, do you want to have a go for it - I'll set you up". So my father approached Kerry Rix and he became tenant of Mill Farm for 22 years.'

In the early 1920s Kerry had turned 70 and he was feeling his age. He had been widowed in 1915 and his life since then had revolved around work. Now, after a career spanning more than 40 years, he accepted that it was time to retire. He would move to Lowestoft and leave the Somerleyton estate to a younger man's care. Kerry handed in his notice to a troubled Lord Somerleyton, who had relied so much on the agent for support and advice. When he pondered over the question of finding a replacement, Kerry replied that he knew of a suitable candidate, and he was already living on the estate.

Captain Walter Wortley Flatt was a Norfolk man, he had been working as an agent before the war but then saw very active service in the Middle East, finally leading a bayonet charge against the Turks which left him wounded but undaunted, and with a Military Cross for his bravery. He was a superb horseman and often preferred that means of transport to any other, riding across country in an upright, dignified style.

Flatt had made friends with Jack Crossley, Lord Somerleyton's second son, and as a result he took on the tenancy of Manor Farm at Lound in 1921. His son Tom adds, 'that was the year the Government scrapped the Corn Production Act; they had guaranteed the price of corn and just before the harvest they welched on the deal. So the result was that grain was half the price and lots of fellows went broke, through no fault of their own. Particularly those who'd been in the war and had just started up.'

Walter Flatt and his wife at Buckingham Palace where he received the Military Cross in 1917

Fortunately for Captain Walter Flatt, he had several other sources of income to keep him going, through surveillance works for drainage boards and crop reporting for the Ministry of Agriculture. Then, at the recommendation of Kerry Rix, he was taken on as the new agent of the Somerleyton estate.

Captain Flatt left some notes of his experiences and he described the scene when he took over. 'Mr Rix was an old gentleman and his means of transport was a pony and trap. During the 1914 war he had lost all his tradesmen and others being conscripted, so that things generally had got behind and my first job was to make a terrier[1] of the whole estate and then a book of tenancies. Up till then there had been virtually no tenancy agreements on the estate -

---

[1] *book of maps*

Lord Somerleyton treated his tenants as gentlemen and he expected to be treated the same.'

Flatt soon set about putting it all in writing. He said, 'This thoroughly upset some of them but eventually, with the exception of one, they signed. The farm of the tenant who would not sign the agreement became vacant and was let at a considerable increase of rent.' Captain Flatt did not go into detail about how that farm became vacant. As far as he was concerned, people had to take responsibility for their own lives, and once a man's working contract at Somerleyton expired, he wanted him out immediately, even if he had nowhere else to go. Flatt explained to his employer, 'After that date he is really a trespasser.'

At around that time he is said to have evicted a family from an estate cottage and incurred the wrath of Savile who apparently railed, 'Never in the history of the Crossley family have we ever resorted to turning anyone out and setting them on the road. That's against our principles.' The details of that event are uncertain, but many families moved on regularly when the father's working contract expired. In October 1902 the headmaster of Somerleyton School had noted in his log, 'Several children left and others admitted owing to fathers changing places at Michaelmas.'

In fairness, employers had to repossess cottages as quickly as possible, to be able to offer a home to new employees. There was no means of commuting then, and a tied cottage was usually part of the deal for farm workers. Even so, there were laws to protect the more permanent tenants and in 1919 it had been Savile who was frustrated when he wanted to sell a farm vacant, but the tenant refused to go. The man's solicitor returned the Notice to Quit, claiming his client's rights under the weighty Agricultural Land Sales (Restriction of Notices to Quit) Act, which had come into force that year.

Captain Flatt was renowned for his habit of riding through the woods and appearing unexpectedly, ready to catch any shirkers on the estate, or local children who might be up to no good. His military training led him to take radical action in 1929 when he suspected an employee of stealing corn and equipment. With the local police he mounted a surveillance operation which ended in them chasing their quarry's van into Norfolk, and finally apprehending him. Before any trial took place, the man was given notice to quit his job and his house forthwith. Later that day, he shot himself. Captain Flatt was alone at the inquest as both Savile and Frank were abroad, but each sent messages of support. Villagers were divided on whether his action had been justified, and a female relative of Kerry Rix offered to coach him on the way to combine duty with sensitivity. He declined.

By the 1930s Tom Flatt was old enough to go with his father on his rounds of the estate, and from his own experience he felt that his father tried his best to be fair minded under difficult conditions. He recalls, 'Farming was of course very badly depressed and around that prosperous-looking mid Suffolk area, some of it had gone back to bush and all these fine houses were falling into disrepair. Farm wages were 30 to 35s. a year and things were tough.' Walter Flatt recognised this and in 1932 he persuaded Frank Crossley, who was by now making decisions about estate matters, that farm tenants should have their rents reduced. That was a difficult time for Flatt too; he was also answerable to Savile, and he had the job of persuading his Lordship that tradesmen's wages should not be similarly reduced.

Captain Flatt seemed indefatigable. For nearly 50 years he did voluntary work on marsh drainage, rivers and coast defence authorities, and later he would be rewarded with an O.B.E. He was also a steward for the Norfolk Show with a particular interest in the heavy horse section. On one of the rare occasions he took a holiday, he went to Jersey, and ahead of his trip Lord Somerleyton gave him a letter of introduction to the Governor of the Island. This led to star treatment for Flatt and a tour of the island's chief Jersey cattle herds, which to some might seem like no break at all, but Captain Flatt concluded, 'This was a very enjoyable holiday and I felt the better for the rest and the change.'

He was a wise man in many ways, and when Savile lay dying in a London hospital, he refused to go and visit, knowing it would be impossible to prevent his determined employer from talking business. Quite rightly, he was proud of his organisational ability and he later wrote about his handling of Lord Somerleyton's funeral arrangements in 1935, when he made contingency plans for every conceivable problem. He was gratified to receive a letter from Savile's son in law, who was then Commandant of Sandhurst. It read, 'In my military work I have had a good deal to do with organising ceremonials, and I therefore know the many details which must be thought of to ensure that things work smoothly. It is with some understanding then that I write to say how well you carried out your duties in connection with today's funeral. It all went off so quietly and without a hitch, and although I know you do not want any thanks, I feel I must say that you could not have served your master better than you did on his last journey.'

Continuing as agent for Frank the second Lord Somerleyton, Captain Flatt was equally loyal and unquestionably trustworthy. During the Second World War he was sworn to secrecy over the testing of amphibious tanks at Fritton Lake. The penalty for giving away information would have been death, and he was only allowed into the area under armed guard. Afterwards, when all the military had gone, it would take some years before the hall and grounds returned to normal and the numerous claims for damages, compensation and cost of living bills were settled. Every detail was carefully recorded in Captain Flatt's idiosyncratic, almost indecipherable handwriting.

A clerk, George Barker, assisted Captain Flatt in his paper work, and after the war he was joined by a young secretary, Geraldine Bailey. She started work in May 1946, and, she says, 'I was only 14 years of age and the first day, I spent a lot of time crying - I felt so unhappy - one day with all the girls at school and the next working with two elderly men! There was no mid-morning break, so I had a cake in my jacket pocket and had a mouthful whenever no one was looking. I was paid 25s. a week, which was probably the going rate for an office junior, and I remember my mother said if I stayed a week, I might like it - and I worked in the estate office for 45 years.'

Mostly Geraldine spent her time carefully writing up rent books, taking dictation, or typing. It took a little while for her to get used to Captain Flatt's clipped, formal speech. She mentions one occasion that still amuses her, 'He dictated a letter to someone and I thought he said the name was "John Hard". I asked him to spell it - it was HOWARD.'

Geraldine settled in her job and came to terms with being the only girl in the office. The elderly men were kind to her and her Christmas gifts from the estate were thoughtfully feminine; handkerchiefs or a headscarf from Liberty's of London. She was excused duty for two half days each year so that she was away from the office when the farm tenants came up to pay at the rent audit; it was a men-only affair when the sausage rolls and sandwiches were washed down with plenty of whisky and beer. In the early 1950s Lady Bridget decided to arrange a staff party, but even then the invitation was only for the males. Geraldine didn't mind, she said she would have felt awkward being invited, but she had to help the maids and workers' wives wait at table instead.

The battle for women's lib. was still some way off, and Captain Flatt's fighting days were over by then; he retired in 1952 and continued to lead an active life until his demise just a few days before his 95th birthday.

Walter Flatt's natural successor in the job of estate agent was his son Tom, whose boyhood years as a troublesome tearaway had long been forgotten. After the war he had given up his job of auctioneering and studied to become a Land Agent, learning from textbooks what his father and predecessor Kerry Rix had gleaned through years of hands-on experience. His fellow students soon recognised that Tom had the edge on them and often checked their theories with his own practical knowledge. He had been lucky in that his father, Captain Flatt, had been shrewd enough to know that the best way for Tom to learn about farming was to be given responsibility on his own land. 'My father was very good,' Tom acknowledges. 'I was a partner on the farm with him and he sort of let it go. He'd seen too many farmers who kept hold of the business so when they died aged 70 or 80, the sons were in their 50s and had never had to take responsibility and were quite incapable of doing so by that time. My father didn't have that attitude of mind, so I was given my head to a great degree.'

Tom's experience and sharp perception were ideal attributes to add to his paper qualifications when it came to working as agent for Frank, the

Captain Walter Flatt and son Tom

second Lord Somerleyton. 'I used to see him usually every Monday morning,' he explained. 'They were all friendly sort of meetings, really, although sometimes he would be annoyed about something or other. He hated the anonymous letter; if he had one from a cottager saying "When are you going to do something about the state of that road" he'd say "If there's anything makes me not want to do something, it's that." If they'd gone to see him, it would probably have been done.'

Tom confirms that his relationship with Frank was blunt and honest.' It wasn't "Yes M'Lord, No, M'Lord". I said what I thought. He'd ask my opinion on things and there was a 'no holds barred' approach between us. That didn't mean he always followed my advice. But he was an admirable man, I thought.' The death of the second baron in 1959 brought an abrupt end to the comfortable arrangement between agent and employer. Estate management was now undergoing enormous changes and, following government advice, the new Lord Somerleyton began to take control of farms as they became vacant, absorbing them into his landholding. In March 1960 the agent's job was handed over to an outside firm.

At around that time, local man Sam Long wrote an article in the parish newsletter about the changes in farming. He looked back wistfully at the harsh old days, from the Victorian era onwards. 'I was born on a farm and after 68 years I am still living on one... it sometimes demands or at least produces 'blood, sweat and tears'. Even so I personally do not crave any other way of life, possibly because I've had no other. My memory takes me back to the early 1890's, before mechanisation had developed to any great extent. Some progress had of course been made; for instance a few hay-cutters were getting about, making much lighter work in the hay field. Scythes were however to operate for many years to come, particularly in places where horses and cutter could not go.'

'I can well remember as a small boy seeing my father's employees mowing barley and chasing rabbits as they bolted from the standing corn. At that time scythes were standard equipment on farms and were often adorned with red handkerchiefs tied to prevent chafing of the hands or wrists. What glorious times we had as children, riding in the empty waggons to the hay or corn fields when harvesting was taking place. The larger boys were very important; they had the job of riding the trace horse and hollering "Hold ye!" Of course, pay was very poor, in fact there was very little money to pay with, that is, among the farming fraternity.'

Haymaking on Somerleyton estate

Many of the farmworkers supplemented their income with turns out at sea, giving rise to one description of them as wearing 'the amphibious costume that corresponds to their occupations, half-sailors, half-farm labourers.' Another account says, 'most of the older men wore plain gold earrings. They used to get their ears pierced when they went to sea as young men for the herring fishing. They reckoned it was good for the eyesight.' There was no suggestion that these men were anything but masculine, and at home the women were just as capable of physical grind to earn a few extra shillings. While several wives could be found in the fields helping with haymaking or down at the brickfields stacking the freshly moulded clay bricks, others were taking in laundry or sewing, or doing char work.

The children were potential earners too; little Arthur Rumsby, at the age of seven, was one of many being paid for scaring crows and the school was often short of pupils at harvest time. They may have missed out on their reading and writing but the practical work experience helped prepare them for the inevitable, as son followed father into the fields. Some can be traced toiling on the land from age 13 to 70.

Monica Crossley wrote about her own memories of the early farming days, when one of the year's highlights was the visit of the threshing machine, which came to process the grain harvest. She said, 'It must all have been very hard work - dirty, too, with the dust and smoke of the engine and the sweat of the men in their thick shirts and corduroy trousers, tied below the knee with a strap or twine, and usually a straw hat.' It was such a busy time that work had to go on, no matter what the weather was like. Monica added, 'In wet weather the men used to protect themselves with a sack over their shoulders. Raincoats were unknown, but everyone wore stout black boots.' She said that women and girls, dressed in white aprons and pinafores, would join in the task of shifting the stacks of corn for feeding into the monstrous machine.

Her father Savile finally bought his own threshing equipment, and a state-of-the-art tractor to go with it. Bertie Butcher had been helping with the farmwork and he was chosen to drive the new vehicle. 'That was right up my street,' said Bertie. 'Lordie bought a Marshall Drum to thrash the corn and I used to hook my tractor on - that was tractor driven - and I'd have to feed and look after the drum. Damn great thing going round, knocking the corn out of the husk. There was a laugh one day when I lost my glasses, and I kept looking in the drum for them. Then Sid Dawes told me "There they are, on top of your head." I was sweating so much, I didn't know what I'd done with them.'

Bertie Butcher taking farm horses to rest

Bertie and his tractor went all over the estate, hauling timber and other loads with a winch attachment, or providing power for the saws at the carpenters' workshop. He had a stocky, tough physique and enormous strength; that was proved when he took up his colleagues' challenge to carry a 56lb.

weight in his teeth. 'I bent down and wrapped an old 'tater bag through it and I picked it up and rested it on my chest - 56 pound!' he said, smiling. 'And look - I've still got some teeth, and now I'm 89. The chap what done it afore me, old Arthur Scrump, well, his name was Rumsby, he done it and that slipped. He lost some of his teeth, said it disfigured him for life. That's what I was frightened of.'

Bertie's career at Somerleyton included countless jobs from gatekeeper at the hall to brickyard worker, gardener and marshman. He did his best at each, although his actions at Herringfleet drainage mill brought him notoriety and almost brought catastrophe. 'I used to go and help down the marshes when the floods were on,' he explained. 'Well, one day I went up the mill sails, I only had tarpaulins, we never had proper ones, and I got the mill a-going and I took the brake off. The old mill was going lovely in the breeze so I went for a walk to the Dukes Head sluice, see if anything was caught in the door. 'Cause people used to hurl bits of wood in the river and drown cats in there, and when the tide went out these things would get wedged in the door. But silly fool, I never opened the sluice door to let the water out.'

'Course, the wind got up and by the time I got back to the mill, the water was backing up and that was going round so bloody hard, it's a wonder she didn't rock off her bed. When I put the brake on, smoke was coming out of the old mill,' He laughed. 'But I got rid of some water that day!'

There were other days when there was no wind at all and the marsh mills would stand silent, so the fields all around would remain sodden. This gave the wildfowl population a great boost, but for the men who tended the cattle on the marshes it was a headache indeed. With what might seem a most unenviable job, the marshmen were some of the happiest. Charlie Howlett, keeper of Herringfleet Mill for 40 years, stayed with his old companion even when she was decommissioned. When he handed over the keys he asked that she be kept in good condition, 'and always keep a clean face on her', he said. In retirement he gave talks to fascinated school children about his love for the lady with four arms. 'She only gave up 'cause her paddles wanted mending', he'd say. 'According to my way o' thinking, in gusty weather with a fair breeze she did as good a job as that 'ere scientific pump. A masterpiece, that's what she is.' In 1958 the mill was fully restored by her new owners, Suffolk County Council; as the last of her kind in Britain, she is indeed a masterpiece. Sadly, her keepers cannot be so easily preserved. Charlie Howlett, who had survived the trenches of the first war and spent countless freezing-cold days and nights with the feisty old girl, died in 1963.

To most people, the marshes around Somerleyton Estate seem inhospitably dank and cold, and at times dangerously misty too. But people who have known and loved the area speak of its shifting moods, its heart-stirring array of light and colour, the soft tang of its salty breezes, and its abundant wildlife. Few were more in tune with the nature of the marshes than Tom Crawford, a man who spent most of his life in Somerleyton and shunned the opportunity to take up a lucrative career on stage in the bright lights of the towns and cities.

Tom had a range of gruelling jobs from crow scaring as a boy to brick making as a wiry young man, and wherever he went, he left an unforgettable impression on those he met. He had been born three years before his mother was married and the family legend tells that Jessie Chipperfield was a servant in a large house until she found herself 'in trouble'. At that time, the early 1900s, single mothers could expect little sympathy or support but Jessie did find a husband who was happy to take on her son too, and as the wife of Ernest 'Kelo' Crawford of Somerleyton, she went on to bear six more children. From the time he could speak Tommy always called himself by his stepfather's name, but, to his lifelong shame, he was in reality Tom Chipperfield.

Tom in stage outfit with fellow performer Percy Edwards

Tom is remembered by villagers as a 'marvellous character'. With almost amphibious ease he taught most of the children to swim in the treacherous River Waveney, whose dangers he knew all to well, having helped to retrieve the bodies of six sea scouts in the summer of 1914. Tom said, 'I would have been 11 years old then. I think this incident is what in the first place turned my mind to the river as I loved the water and was determined to master it.' At the age of 14, Tom rescued a friend in trouble in the river. It would be the first of many lives he saved.

By then, he had left school to work on the fields, but, he said, 'I'm afraid I was a very bad pupil. In the summer it was mostly truant, either to the river or the local orchards. Nothing really bad but I didn't like school.' Tom's shortage of formal education never stood in his way. Like the majority of families in the Somerleyton Brickfield Cottages, the Crawfords were usually just one step ahead of poverty, and Tom recalled that before the 1914 war his mother regularly dished up blackbird pie, which, he added was 'delicious'. In wartime he was often able to filch a loaf of bread from the army stores nearby, and poaching was a particular skill of his.

If Tom was caught out, he usually had an answer for every occasion and it was this sharp-witted banter that eventually manifested itself in the late 1920s as a stage act. Tom, dressed as a country yokel and usually referring to himself as 'Arthur', would tell tales in an outrageous East Anglian accent that had his audiences in stitches. He explained how it all began. 'I was roped in for a village concert by the W.I. I took part in the concert as the comedian. I

had taken quite a few dancing lessons including the latest one at the time, the Charleston, and I slapped quite a lot of this into my song and this brought the house down as they say. This went from village to village and eventually into town. To improve, I took tap dancing as well. I had a very good tutor in town, an undertaker.'

Tom continued, 'I had every chance in the world of going 'pro' in the entertainment world but I never did like the idea, as I liked country life always be.'

The brickyard where Tom worked closed down in 1939 and after entertaining troops and broadcasting during the Second World War, Tom came home to Somerleyton. His wife Dorothy was

Tom and his companion, Joey

a quiet, unassuming woman who was happy to remain in the shadows while Tom basked in the dazzling limelight of his popularity and larger-than–life reputation. They married late but shared an early tragedy. Dorothy had a miscarriage after helping to save her niece from drowning in the River Waveney. The cruel waters proved that Tom could never truly be their master.

The couple had only one child after that, a daughter, Pat, born in 1946. Pat describes her childhood with the man whom everyone admired, but who she knew simply as Dad. 'He took me places – to town, and out in the countryside. 'Course he was marshman and we'd go early, at 5 or 6 o'clock in the morning and we'd row over the river and watch the otters play and that was my early life. He taught me to swim like he did everyone else - chucked me in the river with a rope under my arms and held me up and pulled me in.' Pat says that she was unaware of her father's great popularity, but she knew he had the power to make people laugh and she couldn't help but be acquainted with his unlikely pet – a fully-grown coypu.

In the 1950s the coypu was Country Enemy Number One and it was part of the marshman's job to destroy them on sight. Tom explained that the creatures supposedly escaped from a private collection during wartime bombings. 'This seems to me quite possible,' he said. But he disputed some of the other charges made against the rodents. 'They're dangerous and will attack only when forced to, or if they're cornered. As for stories of them damaging river banks by digging – I've seen no evidence of this, and it would be difficult for an animal that has webbed feet.' He agreed that their reputation for destruction was accurate enough. 'I've seen a field of broccoli go down in one night, and possibly not by more than one coypu. It goes straight through the stalk as a woodsman would fell a tree.'

Tom was highly skilled at catching and dispatching coypus; one spree resulted in 67 corpses in three days, and it made news in the London papers. He was philosophical about his gruesome task, in which he was aided by just two dogs and a stick. 'There are too many,' he shrugged, 'also, the coypu has a habit of coiling up in long grass or sedge and I don't know what the outcome would be if you happened to stand on a large one. It's part of my duty to roam the marshes at all hours of the night and this isn't so pleasant when coypus are numerous.'

He had a sneaking admiration for their tremendous swimming capabilities, and his own pet coypu, Joey, was as faithful as a dog. His friend Clifford Dann relates tales of Tom's concert party days, when Clifford drove him and Joey the coypu to halls where they would be both appearing on stage. 'He used to call it "the old rat". He took it on stage and it just wandered on behind him, or he'd carry it on his shoulder.' Other people still envisage Tom and his large companion entertaining tourists at the local pub, where the amazed onlookers would vie to buy Tom drinks.

Tom's life was not all fun and games but he had a special gift for making people laugh, and he used it to great effect to raise money for charities. He knew all about the cruelty of nature and he wholeheartedly supported the work of the Royal National Lifeboat Institution. They made him an honorary crew member in appreciation of his efforts.

Tom Crawford, or Tom Chipperfield, was a man with two names and several faces. He was a countryman, a clown, and a caring family man. His death in February 1979 left a void in the village of Somerleyton that is still felt today.

Many of the older generation at Somerleyton look back fondly on the days when they knew all their neighbours and spent more time out of doors than inside. There were always jobs to do and games to play, they shared the good times and the bad, and they pulled together. An article in the Lowestoft Weekly Press in 1914 reported the phenomenon of longevity in the village,

A lifetime on the estate (rear, from left) Jack Wilson, Archie Crawford, Egre Wilson, Harry Wilson and Leslie Storey Smith with fellow estate workers (front) Charlie Balls, George Osborne and unidentified colleagues, circa 1930.

and another suggested that 'It is considered unsociable to pop off before you are 80 in Somerleyton'. Even in the toughest times people could reach that target and more, when the average life expectancy was today's middle age.

Veterans of Somerleyton shrug at the hardship and deprivation they have known, and rarely do they envy their grandchildren, for whom childhood lasts much longer, but somehow, they insist, seems lacking in the joys that used to be free. Tommy Crawford often used to reminisce about the old days, and in 1959 he set down his memories of friends past in the poem that inspired this book.

Somerleyton Fifty years ago

Somerleyton little changed; her beauty never disarranged,
Her Parks and woods and rivers too: The village green, a splendid view;
The Railway Station ever clean; Marshes fringed with evergreen.
These with the Street, it so appears, have little changed in 50 years.
Yet going back throughout this time I'll bring into this little rhyme
The village life and village men, or 'characters' who lived here then.
Unlike the beauty they have gone, but still their memory lingers on.
Just take for instance our Co-op, where once stood Mother Fieldings shop;
A nice old lady, old and grey, would always give the seal of day;
And as a fact twas often said, she'd talk nine men and boys till dead.
Whist Drives were then in great demand, these needed someone to command, What better person could there be than Jonty Slater as M.C.?
A cheerful man, well known to all, the wettest night he still would call
"You lose ten tricks if you revoke"; O how he loved his little joke!
Diar Howes can't be forgot, the best known one of all the lot.
The local Tailor, much renowned was known for many miles around.
His customers he'd never fail; he'd traverse marshes, road and rail,
Always gay, alert, aloof, and always used to pad the hoof.
Paddy Welling, Keeper then, perhaps the smartest of the men,
No dog or cat would walk with ease, for Paddy had no time for these.
Dick Butcher, he the boots could sole, or make a broch stick from a pole;
Could rive a bond or fell a tree, making chips fly, big as me.
Foresters Nippers, Dummy, Pinta, Nart, with Giant never seems to part;
With these Ted Darkins also Crow, the woods put up a lovely show.
Stephen Turrell brought the coal. Billy Greig he ran the school;
A grand old chap! now I know why we two could not see eye to eye.
Down Floral Loke then you would find the only villager of his kind;
Blind Billy was as blind as bats, would sit all day there making mats.
Taffy Evans was the Clerk, in the office he did work;

He in the house called 'Nook' did dwell; took on the Sunday School as well.

Between the Chapel and Blacksmith's Loke, the Blacksmith's shop, known to most folk.

The high-pitched voice, yes, all would know, was Master Joiner Eddy Crowe.

At the Church was Parson Bean, to make sure his fold was clean.

And Shilda Roll did toll the bell, could sing a comic song as well.

The Agent then was Kerry Rix, not a soul this man could fix.

With bowler hat, horse, trap complete, a familiar figure in the street.

Of others on the Estate were lots; we'll finish up with Charlie Motts.

Freddy Hanson, Gardener then, knew how to plant just where and when.

With Jimmy Cole no horse would harm; Mays was Steward, Kitty Farm.

The Station then was busier far, though G.E.R. and not B.R.

John Carter was, it so appears, Station Master many years.

Another Character Frank Smith, who's not been mentioned yet herewith;

Daily trips to the post he made, was interested in First Aid.

Jyba who lived on the Green, with Roddy Houghton could be seen

In someone's house about to move the oven, copper or the stove.

There was Billy Wright and Charlie Balls, who changed the colours on the walls.

Jimmy Orford, gay old spark! lived on the Green, enjoyed a lark.

Bob Sturman, he attended cows, whilst at the Hall, was Butler Howes.

The Brickfield too, it had its share, Freddy Garwood who cut hair

In his reed shed, nice and snug; if you moved an inch, he'd have your lug.

Then there was Dan who kept a hoss, seldom did he have a boss.

He too, one time, went round with coal; no, Danny boy was never a fool.

The Brickworks then was in its prime with Rooney driver at the time.

Every Brick was made by hand, the finest facings in the land.

While sweat was pouring down his scalp, on the kiln you'd find Fred Alp.

And making bricks was Harry Long, 'Swepp' always handy with a song.

And yet I'll mention just a few, the Riches Brothers, Johnson too;

Slogging, slogging, all the while, with 'Kelo' burning bricks and tile.

Tom and Dosy brothers were, the land to them did not occur.

Fishing for years far from shore, depression brought them back once more.

Leonard Welton, Rattler Kemp, names like these are not exempt,

Black-sail pirates, both of these, relied upon the sail and breeze.

The Railway too it had its stock, Lonzo, Spuddy, Feek and Brock

Waterson, Ben Rumsby too, Halls and Gowing, that's a few.

Now all these folk from us are gone, yet each one in the village shone.

'Twas folk like these that I would say, made her what she is today.
There's many more are not forgot, space will not permit the lot
If you remember these, you see, you're no chicken, just like me.
Time flies on but memories stay, it seems it were but yesterday;
But looking back, then you will see, it's nearly half a century.

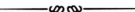

Bibliography

———— ᗶᗶ ————

Isabella Beeton: *The Book of Household Management*, Ward, Lock & Co, 1861

Harriet Bridgeman and Elizabeth Drury: *Victorian Household Hints*, Adam & Charles Black, 1981

Rev. Dr. Edward C. Brooks: *A Thousand Years of Village History*, Trustees for the Parish Churches of Ashby, Herringfleet & Somerleyton, 1983

Audrey and Arnold Butler: *Somerleyton Brickfields*, Trustees for the Parish Churches of Ashby, Herringfleet & Somerleyton, 1980

Tim Card: *Eton Renewed*, John Murray, 1994

Frank Cullum: *Both Sides of the Fence – The Autobiography of a Poacher Turned Gamekeeper*, Tynedale Press, 1987

Frank Dawes: *Not in Front of the Servants*, Century, 1996

Ernest Dudley: *The Gilded Lily – The Life and Loves of the Fabulous Lillie Langtry*, Odham Press, 1958

Jessica Gerard: *Country House Life – Family & Servants 1815-1914*, Blackwell

Adeline Hartcup: *Below Stairs in the Great Country Houses*, Sidgwick & Jackson, 1980

Pamela Horn: *The Rise and Fall of the Victorian Servant*, Alan Sutton, 1996

Geoffrey Howes: *Valentine Quartet*, Redwall Press

Kelly's Directory of Suffolk, 1933

Lesley Lewis: *The Private life of a Country House 1912-39*, David & Charles, 1980

Margaret Powell: *Below Stairs*, Peter Davies, 1968

Frank Prochaska: *Philanthropy and the Hospitals of London – The King's Fund 1897-1990*, Clarendon Press, 1992

Robert M. Pye: *Fifty Years at Herringfleet, 1946-1997*, Tynedale Press, 1997

Eric Webster: *Dean Clough and the Crossley Inheritance*, Dean Clough Publications, 1988

Index

---∽∾---

Figures in bold indicates pages with photographs